insight text guide

Anica Boulanger-Mashberg

Flames

Robbie Arnott

First published in 2021, reprinted in 2023.

Insight Publications Pty Ltd
3/350 Charman Road
Cheltenham VIC 3192
Australia
Tel: +61 3 8571 4950
Fax: +61 3 8571 0257
Email: books@insightpublications.com.au

www.insightpublications.com.au

A catalogue record for this book is available from the National Library of Australia

Robbie Arnott's Flames / Anica Boulanger-Mashberg

Anica Boulanger-Mashberg asserts the moral right to be identified as the author of this work.

ISBNs:
9781922378057 (print)
9781922378064 (digital)
9781922378071 (bundle: print + digital)

Cover design by Gisela Beer

Printed by Markono Print Media Pte Ltd

contents

CHARACTER MAP

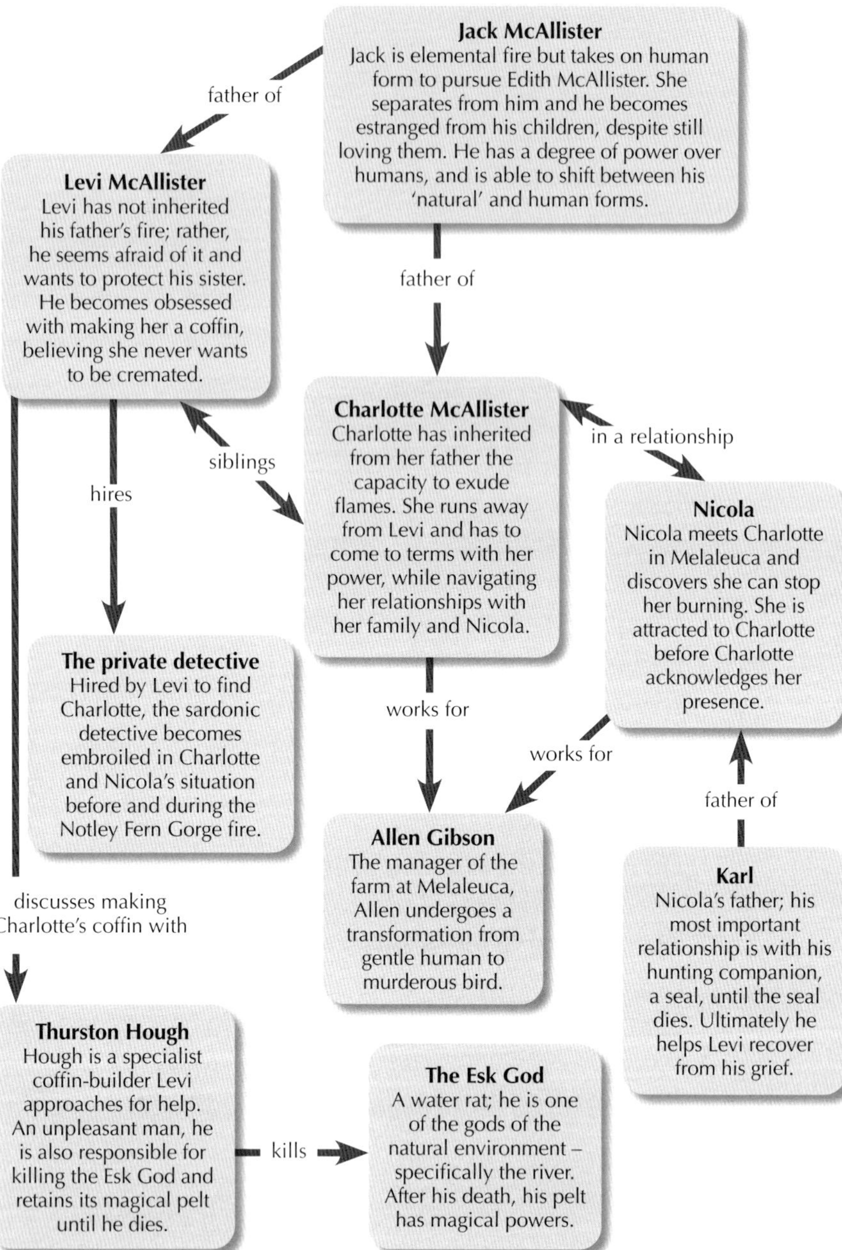

OVERVIEW

About the author

Robbie Arnott (b. 1989) is a Tasmanian writer who has had short works published in literary journals and anthologies such as *Kill Your Darlings, Review of Australian Fiction* and *Island*. In fact, the opening chapter of *Flames* (2018) was first published as a short story. He has also written nonfiction, and was the winner of the 2014 Scribe Nonfiction Prize for Young Writers.

Flames, Arnott's first novel, has been nominated for numerous awards, including the Miles Franklin Literary Award, the International Dublin Literary Award, *The Guardian*'s Not the Booker prize, the Kathleen Mitchell Award and the Victorian Premier's Literary Award. In 2019, he won the Margaret Scott Prize for the best book by a Tasmanian writer in the Tasmanian Premier's Literary Prizes. The rights to *Flames* have been optioned for a television series.

Place is an important element of Arnott's work, not just in *Flames* but also in his second novel, *The Rain Heron* (2020). His writing expresses a strong connection to wilderness landscapes, particularly those in the north of his home state, Tasmania, where he grew up.

Synopsis

Flames gathers a series of intricately related stories, constructing an overarching narrative in which each story contributes an essential element of the plot. While the novel is best summarised by describing the intertwined ideas and events that form the greater narrative, it is also important to recognise the intermittent interruptions provided by the chapters containing stories that seem independent.

In the opening chapter, Levi and Charlotte McAllister's mother dies and, like many McAllister women before her, immediately (and temporarily) returns in a mythical form – merged with the natural world. This sets the tone for a novel that shifts between various genres but consistently relies on magic realism. Charlotte's anguish at her mother's two deaths prompts Levi to plan a burial rather than a cremation for Charlotte, so that she won't suffer the distress he perceives to stem from cremation. This central storyline sees Levi set out on a journey to create the most exceptional coffin he can imagine for his sister.

Charlotte, meanwhile, discovers Levi's plan to build a coffin and flees, misunderstanding his motivation and intent, leading him to later hire a private detective to find her. Charlotte's journey is ultimately one of self-discovery, as she travels to the far south of Tasmania and becomes an almost mythological creature herself. Rather than her essence being revealed in resurrection (like other McAllister women), it emerges in life, and is linked to her paternal rather than maternal line. She discovers that she generates fire from within her own body – an uncontrollable power that is capable of causing great damage, but also counteracts evil, by destroying the farm where she has been working and on which wombats have been dying. The reason the wombats are dying is intimately connected to Allen, the manager of the farm, who merges with a cormorant and becomes a malevolent and bloodthirsty creature. The vast fire Charlotte starts on the farm forces Allen into an old tin mine, where he appears to fully transform into the cormorant he has allied with, but can no longer hunt the wombats.

Charlotte is evacuated from the farm along with the other farmhand, Nicola, who inadvertently finds that her touch can extinguish Charlotte's fire. At the same time, though, the connection ignites a different, figurative fire, driving what ultimately becomes a sexual relationship between the women. They escape together to a stone mountain hut where Nicola knows that Charlotte's flame cannot wreak havoc. In the book's climax, the narrative threads draw together, culminating in a spectacular fire in the gully where Charlotte and Levi's mother's ashes were scattered, followed by a storm and flood of near-biblical proportions that Charlotte, Levi and Nicola all survive, variously traumatised.

Interspersed within this broad narrative arc are other stories that seem tangentially connected but often turn out to be more significant, introducing key characters and motifs. In 'Salt', Karl, a fisherman, learns over many years to hunt Oneblood tuna alongside his companion seal until the seal is violently and devastatingly killed by orcas – later, Karl introduces Levi to a seal pup, in a sign of hope at the end of the novel. In 'Iron', the Esk God – a water rat – chronicles the world of the river, and the harm humanity has done to it, before being trapped and killed by Thurston Hough, the coffin-making expert whom Levi had earlier contacted for assistance. Perhaps the most significant of these interrelated stories is that of 'Jack': pure fire, who travels through time and place and eventually takes the form of a man, for love, marrying Edith McAllister and fathering Charlotte and Levi.

Character summaries

Charlotte McAllister

Charlotte is a young woman and the daughter of Jack, who is flame in human form. From Jack, she has inherited the supernatural (and almost never controllable) ability to create fire. She shares a close emotional bond with her brother, Levi, although she does not truly know or understand him. She runs away from him and works on a farm at Melaleuca, where she meets and falls into a romantic relationship with Nicola.

Levi McAllister

Levi, Charlotte's brother, has apparently not inherited from their father the ability to create fire. After his mother's death, he is driven to build a coffin for Charlotte (to avoid an eventual cremation he believes will distress her) and becomes obsessive about it, to the detriment of his mental and physical health.

Jack McAllister

'Jack' is fire, but teaches himself to maintain a human form for love. His wife, Edith, ends their relationship (and separates him from their children) after learning that he has used his unique powers of influence to induce her to fall in love with him, and he becomes itinerant, in keeping with his true nature. His children grow up not knowing him well and believing that he was a terrible father, never knowing the true reasons for some of his behaviour.

The private detective

Levi hires the detective to find Charlotte after she runs away. The detective is wry, tough and determined, and she eventually tracks Charlotte and Nicola to Cradle Mountain, where she is with them in Notley Fern Gorge at the book's climax.

Nicola

Nicola, the daughter of fisherman Karl, works at the wombat farm at Melaleuca, where she meets Charlotte. She has an inexplicable ability to quench Charlotte's flames. They become friends and then romantic partners.

The Esk God

The Esk God, a water rat, is trapped and skinned by Hough. His pelt retains some sort of mystical power, exerting a hold over both Hough and Levi, compelling them to proceed in their pursuits and providing comfort and strength, but also danger.

Thurston Hough

Hough is an expert coffin-maker to whom Levi appeals in his quest to build Charlotte a coffin. Hough is thoroughly unpleasant and lives in a village where he dislikes others and is disliked by them. After he kills the Esk God, wild creatures plague and eventually eat him.

Allen Gibson

Allen, the manager of the wombat farm, goes from being a kind and gentle man to a mythically influenced, bloodthirsty wombat-killer. He initially loves his job, his surroundings and his charges, but begins to hate the animals (apart from the cormorant with whom he bonds) and the environment.

Karl

Karl, Nicola's father, is a tuna hunter; he and his hunting seal share a remarkable bond until the seal is killed. Karl agrees to try to introduce Levi to a seal (and thus a future) at the end of the book.

BACKGROUND & CONTEXT

Geographical setting

Place plays a large role in the novel and in the lives of its protagonists. *Flames* is set entirely in Tasmania, and while it is a work of sweeping imagination, many of the locations and landscapes depicted are real. Arnott's attention to the details of wildlife, plants, geological features and local communities works to create a recognisable portrait of this island at the southern end of Australia. A familiarity with the general layout of the state might help you to keep track of the characters' movements (for example, Charlotte's journey from north to extreme south) – perhaps find a map of the island to orient yourself with the territory. This will help prevent the possible distraction of trying to envision the various routes described.

Not all the settings in the book are named, or refer to one particular real place – they may be composite landscapes. But there are several notable real locations that play a significant role in the construction of the narrative.

Launceston

With a population of less than 69 000, Tasmania's second-largest city is about a third of the size of its capital, Hobart. Although small, it is urban. Many of the locations in the novel are rural or wilderness areas not far from cities. For example, Notley Fern Gorge is only about half an hour's drive from Launceston. This reflects the closeness between humans and the natural world, while the significant differences in geographical landscapes parallel the chasms between some of the characters (including humans).

Melaleuca

This isolated area in the south-west of Tasmania is accessible only by air, by sea or on foot. It is frequented by bushwalkers as well as bird enthusiasts – it hosts a population of the critically endangered orange-bellied parrot. The wombat farm in *Flames* is an imaginary location that does not correspond to the area at all; in fact, there is no evidence of the farming of wombats as a commercial practice in Australia in real life. (Indeed, several wombat species are endangered.) Nor are wombat pelts used commonly for fur. This is an example of the way Arnott blends naturalism – the detailed representation of the Melaleuca landscape – with more imaginative or fantastical plot elements and ideas.

Cradle Mountain

Cradle Mountain is inside the Cradle Mountain–Lake St Clair National Park in the state's north, about two and a half hours' drive west of Launceston. The park is listed as a World Heritage Area, emphasising the importance of this environment and its native wildlife – both of which are significant in the book. While the place where Nicola and Charlotte first arrive is easily accessible and a popular tourist destination for bushwalkers, Crater Lake is a less common destination in the Central Highlands wilderness, and Oshikawa's hut (which may or may not be based on a real site) is symbolic of Nicola and Charlotte's intense need for isolation in order to find safety. The stark landscapes described form a contrast to the warmth, both literal and emotional, of the women's relationship at this point in the novel.

Avoca and Franklin

These are two small Tasmanian towns, one in the north-east and the other in the south, almost three hours' drive from each other. Each, as constructed in the novel, characterises a small-town perspective; for example, Mavis, the Avoca busybody, describes a place where there are few secrets and everyone knows one another's business. Franklin, on the other hand, is perceived by Charlotte when she arrives as a safe, quiet, 'calm' (p.36) place where she can disappear.

Other real places featured in the book include the highway running north to south, Cataract Gorge in Launceston and the Esk Rivers (portrayed in the Esk God's story).

While you may or may not have heard of these locations, key in analysing the novel are the aspects of these settings that help to construct or shed light on characters, relationships, themes and ideas. For example, Notley Fern Gorge is a real place: a state reserve not far from Launceston. But what is important about the location is the significance it holds for the McAllister family, particularly Charlotte, and the fact that it is the site of the novel's climax. Also important is the way these locations are depicted and written about – always with vivid descriptive language.

GENRE, STRUCTURE & LANGUAGE

Genre

Flames is an unusual novel in that it incorporates numerous distinct literary genres. Taken as a whole, it fits into the genre of **literary fiction** – a type of fiction categorised largely by authorial language choices and engagement with serious ideas. Literary fiction – in contrast to **genre fiction** such as romance or science fiction – is not defined by setting, subject matter or plot, but rather by the tendency towards a more heightened or 'literary' style of language, often drawing on imagery, metaphor and vivid descriptions.

However, several chapters in *Flames* are written in the style of genre fiction, including hard-boiled detective fiction ('Ice'). Together, the different genres combine to create a composite narrative, in much the same way as the different narrative perspectives. Writing across genres allows Arnott to develop characters, complicate relationships (such as those between humans and animals) and build narrative tension effectively by shifting between worlds. Note that some of the genres discussed below overlap closely, and narrative elements and decisions might reasonably be described by more than one genre.

Magic realism (throughout)

The most prominent genre in *Flames* is **magic realism** – a genre that depicts a realistic view of the world but openly incorporates elements, characters and events that do not correspond to 'reality'. Magic realism makes an appearance even in the more literal and realist chapters such as 'Ice'.

A useful definition of magic realism from *The Penguin Dictionary of Literary Terms and Literary Theory* sounds almost as though it is a direct description of *Flames*. Consider elements of the novel that correspond to each of the following genre characteristics.

> ... the mingling and juxtaposition of the realistic and the fantastic or bizarre, skilful time shifts, convoluted and even labyrinthine narratives and plots, miscellaneous use of dreams, myths and fairy stories, expressionistic and even surrealistic description, arcane erudition, the element of surprise or abrupt shock, the horrific and the inexplicable. (Cuddon 1999, p.448).

Examples of magic realism in the novel include:

- the McAllister women being reborn
- the power of the Esk God's pelt
- Allen Gibson's transition into the cormorant; the associated horror and violence; the intensity of his dreams
- Jack's sentient identity as fire, and his ability to take on human form; Charlotte's inherited ability to create fire
- the intricacies of the overlapping and circling subplots
- the juxtaposition of the detective's pragmatism with her casual mention of having seen things like 'thieves who'd sold their shadows to puppeteers' (p.67)
- the epic and miraculous storm in 'Cloud'.

Myth ('Iron', 'Coal')

Mythological storytelling generally presents the origin story of a supernatural being or explains the existence of something in the natural world. Often myths involve gods and their relationships to mortal beings. In 'Iron', the Esk God does not strictly give a history or origin story of his riverland, but he constructs for us a world in which gods and animals interact within particular landscapes. To some extent, 'Coal' also fits into this genre, since it chronicles Jack's origins and history.

Folklore ('Salt')

Several of the stories contain hints of folklore – traditional beliefs and legends. For example, in 'Salt', the heightened connection between the tuna hunters and their seals recalls the Celtic tale of the selkie – a character who can traverse the chasm between human and animal, taking on the form of a seal. Transformed animals are classic characters of folklore narratives, and Allen's transition from human to cormorant also reflects this.

Fairytale ('Ash', 'Coal', 'Feather')

Fairytales are generally stories told to children. The tone and subject matter of most of *Flames* is patently inappropriate for young readers, but Arnott has harnessed some of the traditions of this mode of storytelling, including the incorporation of 'magical' elements such as the Esk God's golden pelt. Fairytales differ subtly from magic realism in that they tend to have a simpler and more defined set of characteristics – for example, they often focus on the adventures of a single protagonist, include elements of magic and have happy endings. In his chapters and subplots, Arnott eschews happy endings in favour of much darker trajectories, although in some senses the book itself can be seen to have a happy ending: Nicola and Charlotte survive the fire and look set to continue their relationship, and Levi appears to be gifted a new purpose in life, thanks to Karl's offering.

Gothic fiction and the Australian and Tasmanian Gothic ('Feather')

Gothic novels take as their subjects dark and often terrifying and morbid examinations of the world, commonly drawing on the natural environment and exploring the supernatural. Sometimes known as Gothic horror, such narratives explore death, featuring themes and tones of menace and melancholy. *Frankenstein*, *Dracula*, *Wuthering Heights* and Edgar Allan Poe's story 'The Raven' are all examples of Gothic literature. In 'Feather', Arnott draws on Gothic tropes in the depiction of the horror of Allen's relationship with the cormorant, and the violence he commits against the wombats, as well as in his changing attitude towards humans and the environment around him.

Early Australian literature often contained Gothic elements, as a means for the new settlers to depict or respond to colonial and penal brutality, the threatening wilderness and geographical isolation. More recently, a subgenre of Tasmanian Gothic fiction has emerged, which 'often reveals anxieties about the colonial genocide of Aboriginal people, and present-day environmental degradation' (Doolan 2019, par.15). These features are clearly identifiable in parts of Arnott's novel: the Esk God's story comments on environmental concerns, and 'Coal' reflects on the 'pale outsiders' (p.176) arriving and taking over from the 'dark apes' (p.41).

Gossip column ('Cake')

The chapter 'Cake' is ostensibly an extract from an autobiography (a genre in itself) but Mavis' observations are more in the style of a gossip column. Mavis is a judgemental busybody with a sense of righteousness about her own opinions. This is one instance of humour in the book, contrasting with and giving the reader respite from the heightened language and weighty themes surrounding it. This chapter also allows for an external description of a character (Thurston Hough) we have previously only seen through his words, in his letters. Mavis' observations correlate with the persona Hough conveys through his incessant insults towards Levi.

Hard-boiled detective fiction ('Iron')

The hard-boiled detective genre, a gritty form that emerged in American fiction in the late 1920s, features a set of distinct and recognised elements. Principal among these is a protagonist who is often flawed and has become toughened and unsentimental due to the nature of their work. Common characteristics of such protagonists are solitariness (sometimes alleviated by sex), cynicism, a determination to find and punish perpetrators, street smarts, a willingness to sidestep rules, compromised relationships with police, and a proclivity for swearing, drinking and using very colloquial language. Arnott's detective is no exception. On one level, she serves as a foil for the more extraordinary characters and events, such as Jack and his story. Yet Arnott integrates this genre into the dominant magic realist narrative by showing the detective's matter-of-fact response to situations such as Charlotte's supernatural fire.

Epistolary novel ('Fur')

In epistolary narratives (told in the form of letters or diaries), events are usually constructed through the perspectives of several individuals – here, Levi and Hough. As well as allowing for multiple perspectives on events and ideas, epistolary writing provides a direct insight into characters' beliefs, motivations and self-perceptions, since it incorporates letters or diaries written in the first person. While characters may be deceptive or unreliable, this form of first-person voice is still valuable for understanding characters and relationships.

Structure

While *Flames* is a novel, it resembles a collection of short stories. This is partly because characters often appear to have discrete narrative arcs within one chapter. For example, the Esk God lives and dies in 'Iron'. However, his story reaches much further into the novel. Beyond his death, his pelt remains a significant motif, contributing to the behaviour of central characters Levi and Hough. Similarly, Jack's story seems complete in 'Coal' – he is 'born', grows up and discovers himself, falls in love, marries, has children, experiences marriage breakdown. But his influence stretches far beyond this. In the early chapters, the connections between stories are fleeting and appear inconsequential (such as Karl meeting Levi briefly in 'Salt'). This inclines the reader to expect the stories to be separate from each other, until we realise that they are all sections of one main narrative.

Further, the fact that in many cases the genre switches dramatically from chapter to chapter (such as from 'Feather' to 'Cake', or from 'Iron' to 'Fur') seems to encourage a reading in which each chapter stands alone. Similarly, the evocative chapter titles hint at their independence. However, the strong thematic and stylistic link between all these titles draws them back together, reaffirming the novel as a single entity.

The narrative structure has a circular element to it. After the short almost-prologue that is 'Ashes', the first chapter tells us the story of Karl and his relationship with his seal. In the final chapter, we return to these ideas and this setting, as Karl passes his knowledge and practice on to Levi, who, as the novel closes, makes a connection with a new seal pup: the novel's final words about this meeting are 'it has kept me afloat ever since' (p.226).

Note: in the first few chapter analyses (see Chapter-by-chapter analysis), a list is included, identifying examples of links between chapters. As these links become clearer throughout the novel, lists are no longer required.

Language

Flames is characterised by rich descriptive language, corresponding to the vivid and imaginative characters, relationships, events and settings. Arnott uses figurative language to heighten the emotional tone of the novel, creating unusual and evocative imagery for his readers, and pushing them out of their comfort zones and into the unique world of the novel. This imagery is often visceral, violent and sometimes frightening, such as in the description of the seal's death, or in parts of 'Feather'. These are examples of some of the figurative techniques used in *Flames*:

- sensory imagery, such as the sound of Levi's axe and of Nicola's head hitting the sawhorse in Notley Fern Gorge, or the texture and warmth of the Esk God's pelt – this connects the reader with the emotions of the protagonists
- alliteration: 'all he knew was swell and seal and spear' (p.20) – the repetition emphasises the regularity of Karl's days before the death of his seal

- personification, not just of animals (such as the cormorant in the early parts of 'Feather') but also of landscapes and elements ('the sky kept thinking about rain without ever making a commitment to it', p.77); this helps us to feel a connection to these elements since they are no longer 'other' but familiar
- metaphor, such as 'a small forest of blue flames' (p.151), which facilitates a stronger emotional understanding of the characters and the story
- non-literal language – e.g. 'the sky was half wiped with the fluff and cream of clouds, but enough yolky heat …' (p.14) – which helps construct the magic realist tone of the novel.

Narrative point of view

Shifts and variations in vocabulary, rhythm (such as sentence length) and tone in the novel reflect changes in narrative voice/perspective as well as changes in genre and style. The relationship between point of view, genre and language choices is an intimate one, as these elements interweave to form a larger whole. For example, the language used in 'Ash' is figurative and descriptive, often relying on sensory imagery – 'her skin was carpeted by spongy, verdant moss and thin tendrils of common filmy fern' (p.1); 'when he reached out to touch her mossy face a crackled lick of fire spread up, over and through her' (p.3) – which contributes to the vivid and imaginative tone of the chapter. By contrast, 'Sky' and 'Wood' are both written in the third-person limited voice, which has the effect of distancing us from Charlotte and Levi, helping to convey for the reader their distance from each other in terms of understanding the other's needs.

At other times, we see events in the narrative from more than one perspective. For example, the capture and death of the Esk God are told in the third-person limited voice, which directs our attention to the Esk God himself while still maintaining a certain emotional distance from the event; the event is briefly described again by Thurston Hough in his letter to Levi. The language choices accompanying these perspective shifts help us to form impressions of the characters involved. In 'Iron', as the Esk God dies, the descriptions are warm, gentle and ethereal, encouraging us to associate similar qualities with the character – 'up he rose, blue sky and patchwork earth masked more and more by the clouds … his river had never been more glorious' (p.47). But in Hough's words in 'Fur', the event is introduced in a clinical and blunt manner: 'a few days ago I trapped an unusually large specimen' (p.58). Despite this section being told in the first person, we are inclined to dislike and want to distance ourselves from the character.

CHAPTER-BY-CHAPTER ANALYSIS

Ash (pp.1–4)

Summary: *Charlotte and Levi's mother returns after her death; Charlotte struggles to move on; Levi secretly vows to bury instead of cremate Charlotte when she dies.*

An epigraph (quotation preceding the first chapter) is always an excellent place to glean information about the themes and ideas with which a text is concerned. In this case, the quote from American writer Ralph Waldo Emerson, known for his lyrical nature writing, alerts us to two key aspects of this novel: the heightened, descriptive and poetic language, and the preoccupation with the natural world.

In 'Ash' we are inducted into a world of magic realism, a genre that will dominate the narrative. The detailed imagery in this chapter sets up expectations for a similar use of language throughout – an expectation that is largely met, despite shifts in genre and style.

This chapter also sees the first instance of a device used regularly in the novel: the harnessing of real locations to host wildly imaginative narratives. The characters (the dead McAllister women) literally merge with their environments, foreshadowing the human–landscape relationship explored throughout the text. In this short preface-like chapter, we also meet an important recurring 'character' (at times a figurative character, at times a literal one): fire.

Links to other chapters:

- the mother's burning (later, we learn about her husband's involvement)
- the coffin (a driving plot element throughout; also connects to a later character, Thurston Hough).

Q Why do you think Levi intends to prevent Charlotte coming back after her death?

Q What other elements of this chapter act as signposts towards the development of plot, characters and themes in the novel?

Salt (pp.5–24)

Summary: *Karl, bonded with his seal, learns to hunt Oneblood tuna; he meets and marries Louise; they have two daughters; his seal is killed at sea and he retires; Karl meets Levi.*

In an apparently abrupt narrative shift, the second chapter introduces us to the fisherman Karl and his family, tracing particularly his long relationship with his seal: his companion and colleague in the dangerous and highly skilled pursuit of hunting the massive and elusive 'Oneblood' (so-named for the 'thick, purple-red artery that ran from their throat to their dorsal', p.9). Once again, the notion of a unification between human and nature is explored, with heavy emphasis on the connection between Karl and his seal: Oneblood hunters see their marine companions as 'the half of themselves they had been born without' (p.6).

The vibrant depiction of Karl's history with his seal prefaces the devastating scene of the seal's death, deepening the impact of this event. Their bond is never anthropomorphised; rather, there is a pragmatic affiliation (the Oneblood hunters work in a symbiotic partnership with their seals) coupled with a profound, enduring, personal and almost mythical thread tying the two together. Once again, the language is often heightened and descriptive, creating for the reader a vivid understanding of landscape and characters. This, too, intensifies the trauma of the seal's death as witnessed by Karl, its 'other half' (p.14). The description of the event is vivid and relentless, forcing the reader to experience the fear, grief and loss that Karl does. The scene also foreshadows similarly disturbing scenes of violence later in the book, such as the murder of wombats.

The connection between human and animal in this chapter is so vital that it dictates human-to-human relationships, as when Karl takes his new partner, Louise, to meet the seal, for 'final approval' before marriage (p.12). Karl is also connected irrevocably to the orcas, the creatures responsible for his seal's death, as he fails to erase the sound of their communication with one another: 'Karl tried to forget that clicking sound. But it was lodged in a hole between his ears' (p.19). Very 'human' sounds – a light switch, Louise's fingers – remind him constantly of this terrifying animal incident.

Links to other chapters:

- Karl crossing paths with Levi
- the Japanese client (whose rock hut later shelters Charlotte and Nicola).

Key vocabulary

Oneblood: a species of tuna that exists only within the world of the novel; its large size means that 'a man couldn't hunt it alone, and neither could a seal, but together they could' (p.6)

Q Which do you find the strongest image in this chapter, and why?

Q How would you describe the tone in this chapter?

Sky (pp.25–37)

Summary: *Charlotte runs away from her home and from Levi; she takes shelter under a dinghy; she avoids a drunken sexual encounter; she travels south to Franklin and prepares to head further south to Melaleuca.*

The focus of the narrative shifts again, from Karl to Charlotte. While the stories are all linked, this is not particularly apparent yet, and the early chapters seem to have only passing reference to shared details.

This chapter is stylistically unusual, shaped by a recurring sentence structure, an example of *anaphora* (the repetition of a word or phrase at the beginning of sentences or paragraphs). These parallel sentences serve not only to echo the relentless iterations of the seal's dying moments in the previous chapter (therefore linking what seem at this point to be separate stories), but also to create a sense of Charlotte's urgency as she flees her brother and his plans. The rhythm created echoes the beat of Charlotte's panicked running; each verb builds tension. The effect is to link us closely with this character, helping us to empathise with her later, during the novel's climax.

The incident in the bar with the miners serves to develop Charlotte's character, conveying her strength and independence: qualities she will later call on for her survival in Melaleuca, in Cradle Mountain and ultimately in Notley Fern Gorge. It also hints at the fire that will eventually explode from her. Here, we see it only as a symbolic representation of her mood: 'somewhere she feels a burst of heat that blazes for a volcanic moment before disappearing' (p.33).

Key point

The calm Charlotte experiences in the placid and quiet town of Franklin (emphasised by the repetition of the word 'calm', p.36) belies the later extremes of violence and destruction that will originate with her.

Link to other chapters:

- the water rat (later the Esk God).

Q Why do you think this chapter is called 'Sky'?

Iron (pp.38–47)

Summary: *The Esk God swims upriver on his monthly journey to worship his 'creator' (p.41), the Cloud God; he is trapped and killed.*

Again, the new chapter is markedly distinct from the previous; again, there is a new protagonist, a new style and a new setting. This one is unusual: the perspective is of an animal, the 'Esk God' – the water rat who slept beside Charlotte under the dinghy at the end of the previous chapter. Their connection links the two chapters even though the action and perspectives are separate.

The chronicle of the creature who calls himself the Esk God is a kind of miniature myth, detailing a god's journey and in the process teaching us something of the lore of the river. The Esk God has 'been here longer than the loud pale apes, longer even than the quieter dark ones who had arrived earlier' (p.39). The length of time (a rat alive today could not possibly have lived before and through the time of white invasion and colonisation) alerts us to the fact that the magic realism of 'Ash' has returned, and this is extended with the relationship between the Esk God and the Cloud God.

The Esk God has no respect for, or need to connect with (in the way that other animals in the novel do), the 'callousness' and 'foul industries' (p.39) of humans; in fact, he despises the harm human activity and progress have inflicted upon the natural environment. However, he does exhibit a close and intense connection with another: his 'high-living love' (p.41) the Cloud God. His desire to be with her reaches a frenzy at his imagined death: 'released from his flesh, he would at last meet the Cloud God' (p.47). His need for intimate connection with her echoes the need some of the human characters show for bonds with animals (such as Karl and his seal).

Links to other chapters:

- sleeping with Charlotte under the dinghy
- the Cloud God (causes the ultimate flood)
- being trapped by a man we later learn is Hough
- his dream of fire.

Key vocabulary

Ben Lomond: a mountain in Tasmania's north-east

Rakali: water rat

Q In what ways does the voice of the Esk God differ from the human voices in the other chapters?

Q How does Arnott shape your understanding of this character?

Fur (pp.48–64)

Summary: *Levi writes to Thurston Hough requesting help to build the coffin; Hough resists; Hough is swarmed and assaulted by animals.*

The correspondence between Levi McAllister and Thurston Hough is humorous – Hough's incessant insults are so exaggerated as to be funny, and Levi's failure to acknowledge or respond to this extreme rudeness adds to the comic tone. This tone contrasts with chapters before it, which are consistently poetic, often bleak (consider the seal's story or the death of the Esk God) and mostly narrated in the third-person limited voice. Here, the words come directly from the characters, so we are able to interpret their motivations, needs and experiences without the mediation of a narrator. The narrative perspective encourages us to empathise with Levi and with his well-intentioned quest; but in Hough's case, while we are invited to pity him for the assaults he faces from the river animals, we have also seen how cruel he instinctively is to others, so we have less sympathy for him.

The links between chapters here begin to grow clearer, as Hough's fate follows directly and inarguably from his trapping and killing of the Esk God in the previous chapter.

Key point

It is not just events that link the chapters, but also description and imagery. Here, Hough describes his 'fingers immersed in the endless warmth of [the Esk God's] fur, while my other hand grips my trusty rifle' (p.64), and in 'Salt' the image is similar: Karl is 'steady with a spear in one hand and the slick scruff of a seal in the other' (p.6). Both these images link nature with violence.

Links to other chapters:

- Hough is the author of the coffin book Charlotte finds in 'Sky'
- the difficulties of the wombat suppliers (pre-empts the troubles at Melaleuca)
- the trapping of the Esk God (recalls the previous chapter).

Key vocabulary

Country Women's Association: the largest women's organisation in Australia, of which Avoca resident Mavis Midcurrent is a prominent member; this indicates that she is community-minded

Cretin: a term of abuse meaning a stupid person

Dilly-dallying: wasting time through indecision

Tumescent: swollen

Wuss: a term of abuse meaning a weak person

Ice (pp.65–93)

Summary: *Levi hires and meets with the private detective; she consults with a police colleague; she tries to bait the miners in the Tunbridge pub and follows Charlotte's trail to several other sources; she flies to Melaleuca and meets Jack McAllister.*

A typical characteristic of detective fiction is the protagonist's eventual success in solving a case, and while this isn't achieved in 'Ice', it ultimately will be. In this way, the chapter is less self-contained than some, as its resolution does not occur until much later in the book.

There is humour in this chapter, and though it is subtler than the explicit language of ridicule in 'Fur', both demonstrate a kind of black comedy – humour derived from ostensibly humourless situations, such as Levi's desperation in hiring someone to find his sister. The humour in 'Ice' has a dry, wry tone, in keeping with the detective's character; her sardonic nature is established in the opening paragraph, in which she consumes a generous shot of gin (p.65).

Although the genre being emulated here is normally firmly realist, the detective makes passing reference to 'off-script' things she's seen, such as 'thieves who'd sold their shadows to puppeteers' (p.67). This helps tie the chapter to the magic realist style of the rest of the novel. It also helps set the scene for when she finally meets Jack McAllister at Melaleuca at the end of the chapter; in a blend of the hard-boiled and the fantastical styles, she experiences a sense of his supernatural being without astonishment or alarm. The chapter concludes at this climax of merging styles.

Q Identify three passages in this chapter that give you an understanding of the detective's personality. Why are they effective?

Q Identify a sentence in this chapter that gives you an understanding of Jack's personality. Why is it effective?

Feather (pp.94–118)

Summary: *The wombats at Melaleuca are dying and the farm manager, Allen, tries to divine the cause; Charlotte and Nicola become suspicious; Allen begins to merge with the cormorant; Charlotte 'leaks' fire; Allen, part bird, is stuck in the old mine.*

The style shifts again, this time to a diary format, offering another first-person perspective, that of Allen. As with Hough, this character is (although not to begin with) distinctly unpleasant, so despite the usual effect of this narrative point of view – to draw the reader closer to the character – we struggle to connect with Allen by the end of the chapter. Arnott creates a tension between first-person narrative intimacy and the fear, anger and revulsion the character stimulates in those around him and thus in the reader. The tension heightens the impact of the character's transition from benign human to savage creature.

This is one of the more complex chapters so far, in that it has a complete narrative arc, where other chapters tend to focus on particular incidents or incomplete stories (such as 'Ice'). It resembles 'Salt', which also traces a narrative arc that can be contained without obvious reference to the rest of the book. However, the progression of events in 'Feather' is much more closely and significantly tied to the development of the overall plot (particularly in the fact that it introduces Nicola and hints at her friendship with Charlotte).

Watching Allen's decline as he becomes the cormorant is particularly unnerving for the reader because of his lack of moral compunction about the events, despite having been an apparently gentle and compassionate individual early in the chapter. Indeed, he seems to gleefully embrace his transition, as when he says 'I no longer feel horror' when the dark dreams 'swamp my sleeping mind, only curiosity' (p.102). He shifts from sharing Charlotte's and Nicola's distress about the wombat deaths to a frightening attitude of taking great joy in his role in their destruction.

Key point

The cormorants arrive and begin to colonise the farm, just as the river animals did at Hough's house, but here Allen welcomes and is welcomed by them, rather than obliterated.

Q Select two quotes from the chapter that show Allen's changing perspective on the wombat deaths.

Q At what point in the chapter do you think Allen understands what is going on, and to what extent does this knowledge last?

Cake (pp.119–25)

Summary: *Mavis Midcurrent's biography lists and describes fellow residents of Avoca, praising all but Thurston Hough.*

In yet another shift of genre, the narrative is taken up by Mavis Midcurrent – who has been mentioned in Hough's letters. Through what is ostensibly a biography, she expresses her views on the residents of Avoca (a village to the south-east of Launceston, on the South Esk River). These fond character sketches – with the notable exception of one significant character assassination – echo the small-town calm Charlotte observed in Franklin. Here we see a microcosm of what rests inside such calm: a world where there is in fact plenty of activity. Mavis' observations are never about nature, except for a passing comment about the animals mauling Hough posthumously; rather, a love of gossip, a very human trait, forms the dominant basis of this short chapter. In this, it contrasts with the rest of the book, where nature is always central. Indeed, the chapter's title is the only one that refers to a human-made substance –

all the other chapters take their name from natural substances and phenomena. Thus, 'Cake' provides an interlude and a reprieve from the intensity of the chapters before and after.

Q How does the humour in this chapter differ from humour elsewhere in the book?

Grass (pp.126–35)

Summary: *The Melaleuca ranger visits the farm and sees Allen has gone mad; he witnesses the fire that Charlotte started; he escapes with Charlotte and Nicola in a plane.*

We see from the Melaleuca ranger's perspective (although in a third-person-limited narrative voice) the events Allen described in his diary in 'Feather'. This includes the death of the wombats (and their subsequent consumption by birds), as well as the dramatic fire started by Charlotte. But the chapter also offers an enlightening view on what might have been happening to Allen. While by his report he was empowered through connection with the cormorant, an external view portrays him as having descended into a 'haggard … froth of madness' (p.129), reminding us that narrative is always subjective. The structure of the novel as a whole emphasises subjectivity, since it continually offers us parts of its story through the eyes of different characters.

Key point

When the ranger sees Charlotte crying tears of flame, he does so 'both understanding completely and not understanding at all' (p.132); this encapsulates well the impact of a magic realist novel on a reader. Events in such a narrative make sense within the context the author has created, but when measured against the 'real' world beyond the novel, they can be incomprehensible.

In the first paragraph, the narrative notes the ranger has 'seen many things that filled him with quiet wonder … He saw it all' (p.126). This echoes the detective's observations that she has seen things stranger than Levi's 'twice-dead relatives': 'you name it, I'd seen it' (p.67). But the events the detective has seen are magic realist, while the ranger lists only natural phenomena. This reflects their characters and occupations: the detective is interested in people more than nature, and the reverse is true for the ranger, who is 'thirsty for the taste of all the wild things in the world' (p.127) and thrives on the 'wonder' of his job in the wilderness.

As the chapter concludes, the ranger imagines the coming regeneration and rebirth of the landscape and wildlife following the fire; he responds to the trauma of his experience by seeing again the 'wonder' he has always found in the wild. Embedded in this denouement of the chapter is a description of him from his mother's perspective. She sees 'in the swaying trees the origin of the man he had become, the things that had grown and nourished him' (p.135); this is another instance of the blurring line between human and nature.

Q When the text presents us with more than one description of events, why might you trust one character's view over another's? (Consider, for example, Allen's versus the ranger's description of their brief meeting.)

Q The ranger doesn't want to tell his mother the 'harsh stories' (p.129) of what happened at Melaleuca. To what extent do you think the stories in this book are 'harsh'?

Key vocabulary

Flare gun: a gun that sends out distress signals known as flares, indicating that someone is in need of rescue; the ranger feels the farmhands may explain away Charlotte's strange fire as a flare

Potoroo: a small, rat-like marsupial related to the kangaroo family

Snow (pp.136–56)

Summary: *Charlotte and Nicola escape to Cradle Mountain; they stay there for a time and their relationship becomes physical; the detective arrives.*

This chapter reflects on the development of the friendship between Charlotte and Nicola, from a third-person limited perspective aligned with Nicola. Their connection is both real and symbolic: as they cautiously enter into a romantic relationship, their strange supernatural abilities form a symbiosis. While the focus is Charlotte's fire (since that is the immediate danger), Nicola's power to quench that fire is also remarkable. Thus they satisfy the adage that 'opposites attract', with each dependent in some way on the other. Nicola feels a 'closing distance between them, the comfort of company, the urge to reach and touch' (p.140). This description could be used in relation to the bonds between other characters in the book: Karl and his seal, the Esk God and the Cloud God, Allen and the cormorant, and Jack and Edith (though this last could be considered more one-sided).

Charlotte and Nicola's escape to a remote part of the Tasmanian wilderness is unsurprising both in terms of character (each had previously made their way to the very remote Melaleuca) and in terms of the book's narrative, since all the significant events and turning points take place in natural environments (consider the story of the McAllister women; the seal's and the Esk God's deaths; the Melaleuca fire). Once there, they are isolated and confined, crystallising their relationship and focusing the narrative on a more interpersonal interaction, though still against a remarkable environmental backdrop.

Wood (pp.157–65)

Summary: *Levi finds the corpse of Thurston Hough, the pelt of the Esk God and the half-finished coffin at Hough's house; Levi's father is in his house when he gets home, and they argue.*

The structure of this chapter mirrors that of 'Sky', with each paragraph beginning 'Levi is', just as the earlier chapter relied on 'Charlotte is'. This has several effects.

- It gives the narrative forward momentum, since each paragraph offers a new action.

- It draws us into Levi's world, associating us closely with his character and experiences.
- It links him with his sister, echoing the sentence structure of parallel parts of their journeys.

The interruptions to the repeated pattern are a small number of sentences beginning 'His father' and a few short lines of dialogue. This emphasises the role of Levi's father in his life: only present part of the time, Jack holds a disruptive power. There are no such interruptions to the pattern in 'Sky', suggesting that Charlotte is more connected to her father than Levi is – which makes sense in the context of her sharing his fire.

Key point

The warm, mystical power of the Esk God's golden pelt brings Levi a confidence and strength that is reassuring to him, but in fact drives him to misguided actions (see p.160). It had a similar effect on Hough, and is echoed in the power with which the cormorant's feathers endowed Allen.

Levi, at the beach, recalls how much Charlotte loved the water as a child, while he didn't (or at least it was Charlotte who did 'all of the swimming', p.162) and that their father never went near it. Levi's memories of the family's relationship with water foreshadow several plot turns, such as the storm quenching the fire, and Levi's ultimate fate, at the novel's end, of being led to the water and put through an ordeal of survival while waiting unknowingly for a seal pup that will mark a new future. However, it is Jack's relationship with the water that is most telling: while we don't yet know his true identity, this clue becomes meaningful in retrospect, particularly when other characters in the book (for example, Karl and the Esk God) are strongly connected to and nourished by sea, river and water.

Key vocabulary

Dolerite: a type of rock particularly associated (in Australia) with Tasmania

Coal (pp.166–89)

Summary: *Jack/fire is 'born'; he lives through centuries; he learns he can take on human form; he falls in love with Edith McAllister and they marry; Levi and Charlotte are born, and Charlotte is imbued with a spark from him; Jack and Edith separate; Edith dies.*

This chapter, like 'Salt' and 'Iron', is a largely self-contained fable-style story. It also constructs a central character (Jack) and contextualises another central character (Charlotte). Jack's story illuminates an idea subtly touched upon throughout: human damage to environments and the importance of conservation. For Jack, the disgust towards humans is particularly reserved for the 'paler people' (p.175) – the colonial settlers.

Jack's story spans centuries, exploring a world more mythical than any we have so far encountered in the novel. As fire, an elemental being, Jack is able to observe the world around him, as well as discovering and learning about the essence of himself; about how he fits into the world; and about his needs, powers and abilities, such as needing to be 'fed' or being able to jump from place to place where there are fires. He experiences rebirths (recalling the McAllister women rising from their ashes) and continues to learn 'lessons, always lessons, strange ideas and stony truths taught to a simple being of flame and hunger' (p.171). As he develops, he begins to have more agency and also more ambitions in the world.

Just as most humans in the book long for connection with animals and the natural world, Jack craves connections with humans and the sense of purpose this brings: 'what part of the world had thrown hooks into his soul? … It was people, always people; only people that he really cared for. He had … come to think of them as not so much a family but as part of himself' (p.172). As an extension of this preoccupation with humans, he begins to pursue his ability to function as one of them and to take human form – the seemingly inevitable conclusion of this is that he falls in love with a human and must try to keep his 'natural state' (p.175) hidden in order to be with her. This calls to mind fairytales such as *The Little Mermaid*, in which Ariel's non-human identity must be concealed from the prince, and it is also a comment on ordinary human relationships, in which compromises often need to be made. As with other fairytales, however, ultimately Jack cannot sustain his human guise and, as the omniscient narrator observes: 'if he'd stopped and pondered it all, down in his brightest, oldest coals, he would've realised nothing good could come from such a pursuit' (p.178).

Q Is Jack's manipulation of Edith justified? What does the chapter suggest about love and free will?

Q Jack is a central character – why do you think we have not been given his perspective earlier in the book?

Grove (pp.190–212)

Summary: *The detective takes the women back to the McAllister house, but Levi isn't there; Charlotte silently resolves to leave Nicola; the three go to Notley Fern Gorge and find Levi; Nicola is knocked out in the struggle between Charlotte and Levi; a fire starting with Charlotte engulfs the gorge; Jack appears and it begins to rain.*

From Charlotte's first-person perspective, the story begins to intensify, leading to its climax. Her introspection about why she ran away from her brother reveals that her motivation was not fear or fury, as suggested in 'Sky', when she bolts from 'a brother who wants to bury her' and take from her the 'family tradition of flames' (p.26). Instead, she claims that, although she and Levi have 'never understood each other' (p.192), she ran away 'out of love' (p.192) because she didn't want to destroy their relationship due to anger at his actions – 'he is the only family I have left' (p.193). (Note that she does not consider her father to be part of her family at this point.)

The role of narrative voice is crucial in examining the contrast between the two motivations for running away. Perhaps here the 'truth' can be read, since the voice is Charlotte's own, while in 'Sky' it is mediated through the third-person perspective. But it is also possible that Charlotte is an unreliable narrator who does not always know the 'truth' herself.

Indeed, she first describes leaving out of love but immediately confesses that she had been thinking of leaving anyway. This inclines us to question her understanding of her motivations. It also invites doubt about her full comprehension of her feelings for Nicola.

In Notley Fern Gorge, when Charlotte's fire eventually lets loose, it is the Esk God's pelt that catches first – the source of Levi's energy and strength. The gorge begins to burn wildly, though Nicola manages to quench the fire in Charlotte herself; the detective tries to revive Nicola in the river; the flames in the humans' immediate vicinity reduce while the fire burns on beyond; Jack appears, and in apparent response the rain begins. Jack is last seen releasing a 'long, heavy sigh', his eyes closed, and Charlotte observes, 'that's when the rain starts falling' (p.212). Although the outcome of this event is left open to interpretation, it seems likely that Jack believes he is about to 'die' for the last time, having just said a form of goodbye to his daughter, and knowing the rain will save his family, as well as Nicola and the detective.

Q Why does Charlotte feel that she should leave Nicola?

Q What is the significance of the fire dying down around Jack?

Cloud (pp.213– 16)

Summary: *The Cloud God unleashes a spectacular storm, beginning at Notley Fern Gorge.*

In this very short chapter, the 'furious' rain (p.213) comes from the personified cloud – see the second paragraph of the chapter, describing the cloud's body, voice and memory. As in many other parts of the book, the line between humans and the natural world is blurred. The fact that smoke from the 'golden-brown … river pelt' (p.215) was what drew the cloud to the area and initiated the storm makes us realise that this is not just a weather phenomenon but in fact the great Cloud God who was worshipped by the Esk God – 'the other half of the cloud's heart' (p.215).

The rain spreads outwards, as did the fire from Charlotte at Melaleuca and at Notley. The storm and flood are swift and dramatic; the imagery is bold and the language choices convey the breadth and intensity of the flood, through words such as *collapsed, raging, howled, snapped, jagged, tantrums, monstrous* and *severe.*

Sea (pp.217–26)

Summary: *Charlotte recounts the events to Levi in the hospital; Nicola convinces Karl to take Levi to the sea; Levi meets a seal pup.*

In this final chapter, the narrative reaches its denouement after the intensity of the fire and flood. It employs a circular strategy, returning to the action of the initial chapters and drawing all the story threads together.

While Levi initially attributes to the pelt the 'strange, swelling confidence' that drove him to the climax of his quest to build Charlotte's coffin, there is another power at play here too:

> … it wasn't just the pelt; even before then, when I'd been pursuing my coffin plan, my memories were murky, as if they were someone else's that had been carefully recited to me … my actions … weren't all that rational. (p.219)

Yet he has no idea what has shaped his behaviour in that way – the dramatic irony is that the audience can infer a possible cause. Jack, who we know has the power to influence humans (as he did with Edith), could have been steering Levi's behaviour throughout. Jack was devastated by having to devour Edith as she was cremated, and does not want to be involved in his daughter's fate in the same way: 'just like their mother, they would eventually die. And he did not want to be close to them when they did' (p.189). In directing Levi to build the coffin, Jack would have been helping to guard against Charlotte's future cremation. Once the storm suffocates the fire (and Jack), Levi is free to emerge from his strange enchantment, and the meeting with the seal pup offers him a new possible future.

Q In what other ways might you interpret the conclusion to the novel?

CHARACTERS & RELATIONSHIPS

Charlotte McAllister

Key quotes

'Yes, behind her pale face there lurks a curious ferocity ... she occasionally seems to lose control of herself in fits of quiet emotion ...' (Allen, p.97)

'Maybe the flames have always been there.' (p.194)

'Levi has probably told her about me and my anger – how I'm unpredictable, how I'm uncontrollable – because I know that's what he thinks: that I am weird and wild.' (p.198)

Charlotte McAllister drives the action in *Flames,* first by running away from her family and then becoming a strange human-fire hybrid capable of great destruction. The daughter of Edith and Jack McAllister, Charlotte was never aware of her father's real identity and does not reciprocate the adoration he had for her from the moment she was born, instead resenting him for leaving her mother: 'her father had never known how to be a father' (p.153). Charlotte's lineage is one in which the females of the family are often resurrected by some unnamed force following their cremation. When she runs away from her brother after their mother's death, return and re-death – ostensibly in fear of his plan to bury her when she dies – we know nothing of her supernatural qualities, and she seems not to either (although she later reveals that she was to some extent aware).

Strong and determined, Charlotte at times comes across as an unreliable narrator, since she is not always fully cognisant of her motivations and desires. Examples of this include:

- when she runs away from Levi, without clarity about where she will go or what she will do (later we learn more; at this stage she is withholding information)

- when she tries to control her fire but is unable to; she is bewildered and overwhelmed by 'trying to summon her flames. Trying to control them' (p.152)
- when she resolves to leave Nicola – ostensibly for Nicola's own good (although this is not explicitly discussed) – but is not initially aware of just how much she does not want to do so.

Similarly, her confession that she had been planning to leave before Levi's scheme because she felt the fire coming suggests that she is not always open and thus, in terms of understanding her, we are at the mercy of what she reveals. Sometimes information about Charlotte's character or motivation is withheld intentionally until climax points in the novel – for example, Charlotte did know why she was fleeing Levi, but readers do not have access to this reason, so we can only interpret Charlotte's escape as a panicked, disjointed flight in spontaneous fear. She runs away seemingly without plans, without intentions and without any sense of what she is running towards. But, as the end of the novel nears, we see that, while she may not have known where to run to, her reasons for leaving her home and her brother were crystal clear to her.

Charlotte's relationship with Nicola is one of the novel's most important, indeed the most active. Charlotte's other relationships are with Levi and (more or less in absentia) with her father. While her family relationships are both troubling to her in their own way – she loves Levi deeply but cannot cope with some of his decisions; she has effectively written Jack out of her life due to his absence when she was growing up – Nicola brings her a kind of purpose and security she has not had before, did not expect and is at first resistant to. Their complementary qualities are at the heart of their attraction, but they develop a bond far beyond the practical: while Nicola quenches Charlotte's literal fire, she also ignites an emotional one, and Charlotte does not know how to manage or control either. At the climax of the novel she, to some extent, succumbs to the enormity of both, letting go of the need for control.

Levi McAllister

Key quotes

'Weird kid ... Tweaky voice, even though his words were smooth ... Even before I met him I didn't trust him.' (the private detective, p.65)
'In a mind like his, grand acts will always trump honest words.' (p.160)
'... a skinny, serious youth, with little sense of fun but a huge sense of responsibility.' (Jack, p.183)

Levi's voice opens the narrative, and his intention to build his sister a coffin is the inciting incident, setting Charlotte on her path of escape and discovery. His desperation to fulfil this quest also allows him to draw other characters into the narrative, particularly the prickly and disagreeable Thurston Hough, who in turn draws the Esk God into the web of the story. Compounding his wild crusade to build Charlotte an exquisite coffin, Levi's connection with the Esk God's pelt, after prying it from Thurston Hough's dead 'skeletal fingers', leaves him 'filled with confidence and a renewed sense of purpose' (p.158). Together, his own drive and the magic of the pelt make him virtually unstoppable.

Levi, though stubbornly determined to see his coffin plan through, is perceived by others as an increasingly unwell and frail young man, driven by an obsession that he sees as kindness and love towards his sister but others recognise as mad folly. When Karl encounters him, he appears distracted and perhaps psychologically unsound, hinted at by Karl's concern for him: *'Mate, do you need any help? ... I mean. I dunno ... Is everything okay?'* (p.23). Rather than telling us directly how Levi is acting, Arnott uses the phrase 'as if Karl was the one behaving strangely' (p.23) to indicate that *Levi* is behaving strangely. Later, his behaviour is undeniably unbalanced, particularly at his crisis point in Notley Fern Gorge.

Levi's relationship with Charlotte is never explored in detail from the perspective of either sibling, but Levi's dedication to protecting her from a cremation he believes she fears – and his blind devotion to his plan, to the detriment of his own health – is a mark of the love he feels for her, made more poignant by the absence of their parents. He believes the coffin will allow him to express that 'he loved her more than he could ever show with words' (pp.159–60).

Jack McAllister

Key quotes

'I don't know much about the guy. Nobody does.' (the Last Graham, p.74)
'... a simple being of flame and hunger ...' (p.171)
'... he wanted his children to be wholly human, like their mother, and not cursed with the eternity of whatever he was ...' (p.183)
'Who would welcome a father who leaves? ... Who would welcome a father like ours?' (Charlotte, p.196)

Jack McAllister is a peculiar character: as mysterious, for a time, to readers as to those who are acquainted with him in the narrative. Jack is not truly human, despite living as a human for long enough to marry and to father children. He is pure fire and retains his essence and some of his capacities even when in human form; for example, he performs for Edith, making fireworks for her (p.185). In this form he remains distant from most humans apart from his beloved, Edith. He even remains distant from his children, despite adoring them (particularly Charlotte). This distance suggests that he never succeeds in achieving true humanity.

Jack appears enigmatic to the humans who meet him, including his own children – who, not knowing his true self, simply feel that he was a hopeless father who abandoned them. He did, but not intentionally: *'there are reasons. Not good ones. But your mother—'* (p.165). Despite his fatherly love for Levi – he 'loved him, tremendously' (p.183) – and his 'awe-blinded kind of devotion' (p.184) to Charlotte, he is unable to inspire them to return this love. Levi 'does not care about the man, not about who he is or what he says or where he goes' (p.165) and Charlotte 'does not trust her father' (p.27).

While most, such as the detective, cannot recall anything about Jack's appearance after seeing him, because he intentionally takes a shifting human form (see, for example, pp.91–2), Charlotte can: 'I've heard people say that they can never remember what he looks like, or that he's hard to describe, as if he has no defining features. But I've always found his smile unforgettable' (p.212). This highlights a certain allegiance between them, and recalls the moment when he cried a tear of fire onto his beloved baby daughter, creating an unbreakable – if conflicted – bond (p.184).

His story is an epic one, of centuries of life as flame, and of his discoveries that he can travel, be reborn (or reawakened) and take on human form. This last he does for love but, problematically, he uses his power to manipulate Edith so that she falls in love with him: 'with a hot snap of his fingers he threw a tiny spark deep into the crinkles of her brain' (p.181). The fact that he 'tinkered with lighting tiny sparks' in humans' minds, sparks that 'persuaded them to look upon him favourably' (p.176), ultimately destroys his relationship with Edith, when she discovers hers was a mind he 'tinkered' with.

Although we do not meet Jack properly until more than two-thirds of the way through the book (in 'Coal'), he is a significant actor in the narrative. It is his fire that Charlotte carries, moving the action forward through the Melaleuca fire to the climax in Notley Fern Gorge. It is, debatably, also his furious motivation that dictates Levi's actions throughout, if we believe that he was influencing Levi (as hinted at when Levi emerges from his frenzy in 'Sea').

The private detective

Key quotes

'I'm no oil painting … But in a certain mood and a certain light I do have an appeal – a flinty, slightly androgynous, I-wonder-if-I-could-handle-her sort of allure.' (p.80)

'I wasn't always like this. You might find it hard to believe, but I used to be normal.' (p.83)

'There is something brittle behind her hard face, her smirked words. Something breakable.' (Charlotte, p.190)

The woman Levi hires to find Charlotte is a classic hard-boiled detective who is uncompromising and determined to succeed, and has the instincts to do so, in addition to a certain lack of regard for her safety, for social norms and for the truth. She knows how to manipulate others to gain what she needs, such as with the 'Last Graham', the miners in the Tunbridge pub and the pilot who takes her to Melaleuca. She lives alone, has no concern for aesthetics – 'I'm not interested in pretty things' (p.66) – and has apparently no sense of purpose other than in her work, claiming (perhaps disingenuously), 'I don't feel much at all' (p.84). The fact that she is referred to by a job title rather than a name enhances the notion that she exists only for her work.

The detective is one of the most realist characters in the book – there is little that is supernatural about her story or her actions, despite the passing comment 'you name it, I'd seen it' (p.67) in reference to paranormal events. She provides a contrast with characters such as Jack, Allen and Charlotte, who are not completely human. However, although she claims to have 'no hidden talents', she exists not entirely apart from the novel's dominant magic realism. She has an 'enhanced ability' to sense things about to go wrong, and claims it is 'pretty accurate ... it's a twinge I can trust, and I usually listen to it' (p.76). She experiences this when she meets Jack – perhaps the least realist character in the novel, so theirs is an encounter of two different worlds.

Nicola

Key quotes

'... she caused that summer smile ... She split the face he showed the world, and drew his love towards her.' (Karl's view of Nicola, p.137)

'And Nicola – who was always so measured, so thoughtful, so full of plans and logic and duty – was standing up and following her.' (p.138)

'... she had lived by putting others first. Her first instinct was always to help, to shrink back from the front and push others forward ... she drew pleasure from how she could affect others.' (p.145)

Nicola is introduced briefly in 'Salt' as Karl's young daughter, and then as an eighteen-year-old who intends to become a vet, and who, when her mother takes the family to Melaleuca, 'became so wide-eyed and enamoured with the place that she didn't want to leave', while her father could not understand 'what his daughter's soul was touching' (p.21). This establishes her connection with the natural world and with Melaleuca in particular; she remains there while studying her veterinary degree, subsequently taking Charlotte to Cradle Mountain and then following her to Notley Fern Gorge – no longer the place of 'glistening greenness' (p.21) that she visited as a child, but a site of great danger that she only just survives.

Nicola's friendship with Charlotte overcomes an inauspicious beginning, when Charlotte appears to have no interest in her after arriving at Melaleuca. Nicola had hoped for 'a friend. At the very least, someone to talk to' (p.139), and later she hopes gently for more – she feels an 'urge to reach and touch' (p.140) – but Charlotte is entirely uninterested in companionship. It is not until the crisis prompted by Allen's madness that Charlotte and Nicola truly connect; then Nicola discovers that just by touching her, she can halt the flow of Charlotte's blue fire, and therefore defend what is around them, as well as defending Charlotte.

Once they escape Melaleuca, Nicola becomes extremely protective of Charlotte, at first keeping watch over her in order to arrest any flames. Soon, when they begin to sleep in the same bed (so Nicola can be nearby if she is needed), Charlotte's fire calms a little and stays silent for days. This symbolises Nicola's friendship as a salve for Charlotte's grief and pain (represented by her fire). It is a resurgence of fire that initiates the women's sexual relationship, when Nicola's protective touch becomes a source of mutual desire.

The Esk God

Key quotes

'A swimmer; a feaster; a bright thief; an oversized native water rat.' (p.29)
'But the Esk God remained, and the Esk God thrived, for who could kill a river?' (p.44)
'It is a truly wondrous pelt ...' (Thurston Hough, p.58)

Like Jack and (for part of 'Feather') Allen, the Esk God provides a non-human perspective on the natural world. We are at first encouraged to find his perception of himself as a 'god' mildly amusing, since we have already met him from Charlotte's perspective as an innocuous water rat who sleeps beside her for warmth under the dinghy, and does not bother to 'flee or squeak or bite' but rather 'curls back to sleep' (p.29) when she leaves. He has an apparently inflated sense of his own value and significance, and the two versions of him are very much at odds, offering a comment on the intermittent compatibility between nature and humans. This contrasts with other relationships within the novel, such as that between Karl and his seal, or the morbidly symbiotic union between Allen and the cormorant.

Soon, however, the Esk God's authority and abilities within the river begin to emerge as genuine, making his status as a god quite convincing. He has supernatural powers to see beyond the 'real' around him; for example, he knows bizarre things about humans that they themselves may not – 'he knew that some of them ... grew horns from their temples (horns their fellow apes could not see), some cried tree sap, some licked lips with bladed tongues and some, like the warm-stomached girl, returned after their ash had been scattered into the winds' (p.40). He is passionate about his dominion and scornful of the impact 'hateful' humanity has on the natural world; before humans, 'everything in the land and water had consisted of a wider grandness' (p.43).

In contrast to his view of humans, the Esk God maintains an extraordinary veneration of and love for the Cloud God, pilgrimaging to worship her every month, even though he has never caught 'a glimpse of her face' (p.43). Later, during the storm scene, we learn that this love is reciprocated.

The Esk God also has an innate awareness of the relationships between elements of nature – all the various Gods (the Shale God, the Bark God and so on) exist within an equilibrium, each determining the fates of their own areas of influence. Within this microcosm, the Esk God considers himself 'in charge' (p.39): 'central to his duties was keeping life in the river in balance' (p.45). His capture and death is a reassertion of the human dominance he has critiqued.

Fittingly for a god, after his death the Esk God's pelt retains a remarkable power and hold over the humans who come into contact with it; it magically keeps its softness and its warmth ('even when laid outside under a winter moon', p.58) and brings a strange mixture of comfort and power to anyone who holds it. Both Hough and Levi are bewitched by it, and driven to actions that are not necessarily positive; for example, the power Levi feels when he has it with him supercharges his wild quest to build the coffin, ultimately leading to disaster in Notley Fern Gorge. Even Charlotte senses its power when she briefly holds it: it 'glows' (p.208). Again, this suggests that the Esk God really is godlike, able to influence humans even after his death.

Thurston Hough

Key quotes

'I am convinced that you are the only man who will truly understand what I mean and what I require.' (Levi, p.49)
'… all I ask of the world is that it leaves me alone.' (p.50)
'He was a terrible neighbour, an unpleasant person and a poor citizen.' (Mavis, pp.124–5)

The reclusive Hough is one of the less complex characters in the novel, and does not undertake a particular journey. His significance in the narrative is primarily in facilitating several important plotlines: Levi's coffin quest and the Esk God's death. He is a comical caricature, and his hyperbolic, graphic insults in his correspondence with Levi not only emphasise the extent of his unpleasantness but also introduce a glimpse of levity into an otherwise intense novel. He evinces the 'greed, horror and dirt of people' (p.85) that the detective refers to and the Esk God despises.

His language is formal ('I have built myself a quiet life of monastic contemplation', p.50), aggressive ('you parasitic swineherding subhuman mongoloid', p.50; 'Quivering Pile of Irritation Made Human', p.63; 'disgustingly promiscuous old crone', p.52) and dismissive ('do not contact me again', p.50), painting a portrait of a man keen to distance himself from human connection and emotion.

Allen Gibson

Key quotes

'Having failed to meet the right woman I do not have children of my own, and this herd of wombats is the closest thing to family that I might ever know.' (p.96)

'... he'd gone mad. Cruel. Wrong.' (Charlotte and Nicola, p.128)

'A quiet man, but a sane one. A good farmer. A friend ...' (the ranger, p.128)

Allen Gibson, the manager of the Melaleuca Farm Estate wombat farm, undergoes one of the most dramatic transformations in the novel – perhaps even more dramatic than Charlotte's discovery of her ability to create fire. His change is not only of attitude but also of personality and appearance. The transition is mainly communicated through his diaries, although there is a dramatic irony in the fact that he does not seem to perceive his intense changes as remarkable. He realises that he has a growing power – 'I did feel something. I felt joy. I felt power. I felt the giddy swirl of freedom' (p.108) – but has no awareness that he has gone from being a gentle man, who appreciates his farmhands and loves the wombats he cares for, to a malicious and bloodthirsty murderer. This transition can be traced through 'Feather' in the shifts in language, tone and content, including his attitude towards Nicola and Charlotte, as well as towards the cormorant. See below for some examples.

- Allen says, 'Obviously I am not killing the creatures' (p.96); yet later he reveals, 'I remembered … going straight for the burrows and killing with firm purpose' (p.111).
- He says, 'The situation is perplexing and upsetting – I must admit that the deaths are taking a significant toll on me. Over the years I have formed a strong bond with the wombats' (p.96); but later he describes them as 'four-legged lumps of uselessness made flesh … I must always have hated them' (p.107).
- While he says, 'this place is my home … I won't be leaving the lonely beauty' (p.98), later he resents 'all the long years I have been trapped in this barren southern hell' (p.107).
- Allen's 'dark, flickering dreams' send 'a nameless horror clattering through' his soul (p.99); but later they 'have been robbed of their menace' and he 'no longer feel[s] horror … only curiosity' (p.102).
- He does not like to 'go near' the cormorant, finding it 'loathsome' (p.95), but later he records that the joy at its presence is 'the richest moment of happiness I have ever experienced' (p.110).
- He begins to feel that Nicola and Charlotte are 'plotting' and says 'where I once admired them, now I regard them with suspicion' (p.101). (Later, from Nicola's point of view, we see others suspicious of him instead.)

As with Levi earlier in the book, Arnott conveys Allen's mental state indirectly. Allen is apparently unaware of his condition, later described as madness – the ranger asks if he is 'feeling unwell' and if he needs 'a doctor' (p.107), reassuring him, *'you aren't yourself … we'll sort all this out'* (p.108). Thus Allen is another unreliable narrator: his knowledge of himself is not as objective as that of the reader. This echoes the deterioration of Levi's mental stability.

Karl

Key quotes

'Men from the north coast of this southern island – muttering men, salt-rinsed men, men like Karl – had been hunting this way since before records of the coast were kept.' (p.6)

'The seal rested, the waves chopped, and the true meaning of salt and water and air wobbled inside Karl's mind.' (p.7)

'After work, after helping his parents around the house, Karl was always back out in the water with his seal.' (p.9)

Karl is a secondary character in the narrative, and while his story is not fantastical in style or content like others, it is filled with a kind of ordinary magic: the connection he has with his seal. The two are not just hunting companions but joined at some spiritual level, and share a kind of unspoken love. The fishermen from the north coast of Tasmania see their seals as 'the half of themselves they had been born without' (p.6); Karl considers his seal 'his other half' (p.14). Karl's first meeting with his seal is almost romantic, as they stare for a long time into each other's eyes and the pup 'leaned in to his grip and rested a slippery cheek and a comb of wiry whiskers against the lines of Karl's palm'; the second time, Karl sees the pup's eyes staring 'once again into his own' (p.7). This remarkable partnership dominates Karl's life – to the extent that it is important that his seal approves his choice of Louise as a wife.

The death of Karl's seal is a trauma from which he never recovers, and the fact that his daughters are not interested in fishing increases his disconnection from tuna hunting. However, his chance meeting with Levi (pp.22–4) is a precursor to the final chapter, when Karl re-enters the narrative through Nicola and the Notley fire. His actions tie the story together, even though he is largely absent throughout it. This structural choice brings coherence to a fragmented narrative. Just as Karl once waited for his seal, he takes Levi to the sea and forces him to wait, without explanation, for a meeting. Karl facilitates Levi's healing in that moment, but it also provides a form of closure for Karl, as he passes his legacy to someone who needs it.

THEMES, IDEAS & VALUES

Connections and pairs

Key quotes

'… the half of themselves they had been born without …' (of hunters and their seal companions, p.6)
'… this herd of wombats is the closest thing to family that I might ever know.' (Allen, p.96)
'The glorious cormorant did reach me; it touched me; it *joined* with me.' (Allen, p.112)
'… centuries of mutual, touchless admiration.' (of the Esk God and the Cloud God, p.215)

Nearly every character in this novel craves some form of deep connection with another, with the exceptions of the detective and Thurston Hough (although his connection with the Esk God's pelt could be seen as a version of such a craving). This does not necessarily mean love – although in the cases of Jack and Edith, and Nicola and Charlotte, romantic love is part of the desire to be with another. Nicola, for example, desires Charlotte 'with an intensity that she couldn't remember feeling before: a white-churned feeling of fear and sorrow and urgency' (p.155). Their relationship emerges from an inexplicable connection between the ability to create fire and the ability to quell it. Platonic love, too, is sometimes what characters seek out, such as that between Karl and his seal, or between Levi and Charlotte.

Relationships often take unusual forms in *Flames* and cannot be classified in terms of simple companionship. For example, there is a tie between the Esk God and the Cloud God; he reveres and cherishes her, and she feels similarly about him. She is 'his creator, his meaning, his life' (p.41), and he craves closeness with her – 'his love for her was not a love of choice; he loved her infallibly' – even though she is a mystery to him and he has 'never even seen her' (p.41). Their connection is as deep as the love between any of the human partners, and perhaps even more so, when measured by the scale of the Cloud God's fury in the penultimate chapter: a storm born of her grief at the loss of 'her waterlocked love' (p.215); a storm 'made of sorrow' (p.216).

The relationship between Jack and Edith is similarly difficult to classify. Edith's love for Jack was kindled supernaturally: it was Jack's interference in her thoughts that led to her attraction to him. Thus, their love was based on a power imbalance, his need rather than hers (although later it is she who proposes marriage). His desire for her was 'an obsession born and chased' (p.178). A symbolic reading of this relationship might take Jack's 'control' of Edith's mind as simply the human experience of love, of being caught up by someone and feeling compelled by and drawn to them. Whether literal or symbolic, the relationship represents a strong desire to couple – at least from Jack's, and partly from Edith's, side.

Human and animal

Karl's relationship with his seal is a bond of function: a seamless team, they have built their collegiality over time. But Karl becomes so closely tied emotionally to his seal that its death devastates him. He has lost 'his partner', 'his other half' (p.14). He seems to also lose a sense of purpose, and 'didn't have the energy or appetite to start the training process' with another seal, even though other hunters 'had successfully re-partnered' (p.19). While we lack access to the seal's thoughts, there are hints that there is at least some reciprocity: when they first met, they 'locked eyes', and the pup 'leaned in to his grip and rested a slippery cheek' on Karl's hand (p.7); and before the orca attack, the seal 'protected' (p.18) Karl. Their success in hunts is evidence of the tight bond they share and their remarkable capacity to work together as a 'tuna team' (p.10). Even Karl's human partner, Louise, must first meet with the seal's approval.

The animal–human relationship between the cormorant and Allen Gibson is more malignant. At first there is animosity – at least from Allen, as he does not trust the bird and stays far from its territory. But soon it becomes a controlling relationship, as the bird begins to take over Allen's dreams and then his body, making him become angry, dangerous, deluded and eventually trapped in a tin mine – although ultimately, during the epic storm, 'something foul and broken, limp and swollen, something built with flesh and feathers' (p.214) flies out of the mine, so he apparently survives in some form. But he has given over control of his human body, and his humanity, to the 'glorious cormorant' (p.109, p.112, p.113, p.116, p.117) and in doing so has become a monster. Whether this chapter is taken literally, or as a metaphor for Allen sliding into some form of mental illness, the representation of that mutually dependent relationship is still a comment on the sometimes problematic desire to merge with another creature.

Humans and the natural world

Key quotes

'... in years past everything in the land and water had consisted of a wider grandness.' (p.43)
'It was spectacular, I suppose, in the way that nature often is ...' (the detective, p.90)
'It was as if she was trying to blend in with the fields and snow.' (p.139)

The relationships between humans and the natural environment around them is foregrounded in *Flames,* and the majority of the action takes place outdoors. In the very beginning, we see a literal uniting of the two, as the McAllister women come back after death, merged with the 'landscape that had re-spawned them' (p.3): Edith is part fern; Charlotte and Levi's grandmother, a collection of marine entities; others, 'fused with leaf and lichen, root and rock, feather and fur' (p.2). This sets the tone for a text in which the boundaries between human and environment are porous and fragile. This is nowhere more obvious than in the bonds between humans and animals, but it is also explored in humans' connection to landscape.

However, the connection is fraught. At numerous points we see nature and humanity at odds. An example is the sea animals who 'plague [Hough's] doorstep' and ultimately destroy his body after his death (for which they are likely responsible); it is as though nature is punishing him for his murder of the Esk God, for breaking some sort of balance in the natural world. This corresponds with views we see both from the Esk God and, later, from Jack. The Esk God despises white settlement and its increasingly negative impact on his environment. Jack – in his fire form, representative of the natural world – similarly judges humans, particularly European settlers or the 'paler people', for the damage they do to the land, 'in ways he could not have imagined' (p.175). Allen, too, comes to detest 'meddling contraptions of machinery or human design' (p.105). However, Jack also longs to be part of the human world rather than his own, exemplifying the inextricable connection between the two, while also questioning humans' ability to coexist peacefully with nature – there is a sense that Jack must choose to which world he shows his allegiance, as he cannot successfully straddle both.

Key point

The relationship between humans and nature has always been uneasy, with humans often impinging on and destroying nature. This is represented most clearly in the death of Esk God, a custodian of the river who 'had been here longer than the loud pale apes, longer even than the quiet dark ones who had arrived earlier' (p.39). The line 'but the Esk God remained, and the Esk God thrived, for who could kill a river?' (p.44) proves an example of dramatic irony, given that it precedes the Esk God's physical demise.

Alienation and isolation

Key quotes

'I have built myself a quiet life of monastic contemplation … all I ask of the world is that it leaves me alone.' (Hough, p.50)

'Here I have found the solitude that I have been searching for my whole life.' (Allen, p.117)

'The sadness in these eyes … the sorrow leaks like tears or blood.' (Charlotte on Jack, p.212)

While much of the novel explores ideas of deep connection and bonding, their opposites – isolation and escape – are also important themes, partly in the way that the two themes illuminate each other.

Alienation and loneliness

The complicated relationship between Charlotte and Levi separates rather than unites them. As early as the first chapter, we see a fissure in their ability to decipher the other's needs. Levi finds Charlotte's grief 'worrying' (p.4) but does not talk to her about this, and later Charlotte admits: 'I could have spoken to him, but he would not have listened' (p.193). This seems poignant in light of her deep feelings: 'between us there is love … love built with his stubborn resolve, with my hot temper, with all the care our mother poured into us' (p.192). There is a cautious resolution between them by the novel's end; Levi accepts it when Charlotte tells him she 'would forgive … probably, in time' but he cannot respond – 'I was going to say something, I don't know what' (p.220) – showing that, even after the dramatic denouement in Notley Fern Gorge, they still struggle to communicate their feelings, even as they come to understand their love for each other.

Loneliness can also be alienating, and can lead to great distress. In Levi's blind devotion to building the coffin, he blocks out the world around him and becomes profoundly isolated, rejecting even tentative enquiries after his health (such as when Karl meets him briefly, at the end of 'Salt'). He reaches out only to Hough and the detective, individuals to whom he has no connections beyond their professional engagement. This seclusion is to his detriment: he degenerates quickly into an unhealthy mental and physical state. Levi is obsessive, antisocial and withdrawn, and stops eating properly, becoming 'malnourished' (p.22), 'skinny' (p.66) and eventually 'emaciated' (p.205); his hair is 'long and knotted … greasy' (p.205) and his 'once-white teeth, always meticulously scrubbed' are 'covered in a grey-green film' (p.206).

Similarly, Allen Gibson, already living in a remote location, slides into a 'froth of madness' (p.129) as his reality deteriorates into wild dreams and beliefs (although the novel leaves the truth of Allen's transformation, like many other paranormal events, open to interpretation). He is no longer rational: he threatens his former friend, the ranger; he becomes violent and dangerous. As seen through the eyes of Charlotte and Nicola and then the ranger, in his psychological isolation (which echoes his geographical isolation) Allen has 'gone mad. Cruel. Wrong' (p.128).

Solitude

Seclusion in *Flames* is not always negative, however. Sometimes it is chosen. Even in 'Feather', it is difficult to definitively identify a causal relationship between Allen's madness and his isolation. Is he left alone at Melaleuca (and subsequently in the tin mine) because he has become unhinged and so has frightened people away? Or was it his desire for solitude that pushed him to defend his territory violently and wildly? If we believe his diaries, he hates Nicola and Charlotte, and even the ranger (who considered Allen 'the closest thing to a friend he had down here', p.129), and wilfully drives them away from Melaleuca, his emotional isolation breeding more intense physical isolation. Indeed, he has previously expressed his great love for Melaleuca, never wanting to leave the remote landscape, with its 'gathering sense of wild solitude that breathes out of every crack': 'I won't be leaving the lonely beauty of this place; not if I can help it' (p.98).

As Allen's transformation progresses (whether that be interpreted as moving into a state of delusional loneliness, or truly a cross-species transition), he becomes more and more at peace with himself and his surroundings. After the farmhands have left, he declares, 'at the sight of the empty farm ... A feeling of calmness settled over me' (p.108), and when he is in the mine, he claims to have 'found' the solitude (p.117) he has always desired.

The detective, too, seems to enjoy her own company. Her life revolves around her work, and she has cultivated an emotional numbness that keeps her at arm's length from others. She maintains acquaintances – such as the senior detective, the Last Graham and Cindy the pilot – apparently only to the extent that they are useful to her. Her sole companion in life is a cat, and it is not even her own but a neighbour's, which represents the extent of her loneliness. Her passing mention of her fiancé cheating on her suggests a possible reason for her decision to isolate herself socially, and while it obviously works for her, it is possibly one of her maladaptive coping mechanisms (she acknowledges that she blocks things out by drinking). In this, there are parallels with Levi's refusal to confront his own grief.

Another character who has intentionally isolated himself is Thurston Hough. He is horrified when Levi tracks him down; he considers even the delivery of mail an 'invasion of his privacy' (p.122). But in the end, his isolation means that there is nobody to protect him when the animal assaults begin to intensify, and not even any relatives to identify his body.

Key point

Solitude and isolation can sometimes be protective, such as when Nicola takes Charlotte to Cradle Mountain.

Death, loss and grief

Key quotes

'… the tears were flames, and they were coming from within Charlotte.' (p.132)

'… the fire, having razed the vegetation, would have burned itself out … new shoots would soon spring forth, green and vital, stronger than before.' (p.134)

'Our mother's ash was still floating before my eyes … and his plan to make me a coffin was too much death for me to deal with.' (Charlotte, pp.192–3)

The narrative begins with a death, but at the same time, in that very first sentence, we are introduced to the idea of rebirth: death is not always an end point. In 'Ashes', many of the McAllister women return after their deaths, but transformed; this is an idea revisited throughout the novel. Death also shapes the narrative in the sense that the overarching journey is of Charlotte and Levi, each in their own way, coming to terms with their mother's death.

For Charlotte, Edith's death is devastating. She 'struggled to move on' and small things 'threw her into fits of uncontrolled screaming' (p.4). (This behaviour is echoed later, when the wombats at Melaleuca are dying and Charlotte 'cannot look at them; she retreats to the farthest part of the farm to scream, and scream, and scream', p.97.) Even as the novel heads towards its conclusion, still she is tied to that memory of having to let go of her mother, the moment when she spread Edith's ashes in Notley Fern Gorge: 'I was scraped hollow with the loss of her' (p.201). It is possible to interpret her entire journey – running from her home, isolating herself at Melaleuca, starting the huge fire, returning to Notley Fern Gorge and starting the fire there – as a passage through grief. In such a reading, Nicola can be seen as a soothing balm for her, extinguishing the fire that is grief; the cathartic storm in 'Cloud' may represent a cleansing and mark an end to this period of sadness. She, Levi and Nicola all survive the fire in the very place her mother's ashes were scattered, and she emerges, just as Levi does, into a next phase of life – a version of rebirth.

Key point

Rebirth through flame, such as the McAllister women experience, is a common motif in various literatures and folklore. An example is the mythical phoenix, a bird said to live for hundreds of years before burning itself and emerging from the fire as a young creature ready to live through another cycle. The phoenix often serves as a symbol of eternal life.

Levi channels his mourning into his attempt to help his sister interrupt the cycle of cremation and rebirth – a rite of passage Charlotte has not actually expressed a wish to avoid. In setting off on his feverish quest to build her a coffin, he refuses to confront his own grief, instead transferring his emotions onto Charlotte when he thinks she, not he, needs '*help*' (p.207). Of Edith's death, he claims in an offhand way, 'I quickly got over it' (p.3). He attributes his dread of Charlotte's eventual resurrection to his belief about her suffering, rather than recognising that he is plagued by 'endless, and worrying … thoughts of our mother, burning to ash for the second time' (p.4). His unresolved grief intensifies, and in the harrowing climax in the gorge his actions almost lead to the death of the other important woman in Charlotte's life: Nicola. He only begins to let go of his sadness when Karl introduces him to a seal pup and he sees a future for himself in which he is newly buoyant.

The potential relationship with the seal also represents a cyclical view of life and death, since it brings the narrative back to the shattering experience of death in 'Salt'. The explicit and shocking description forces the reader to share Karl's trauma and grief, but in the final chapter when he (at his daughter's insistence) passes on a symbolic baton to Levi, a rebirth occurs for him.

A similar representation of rebirth is in the Esk God's story. While his death is vivid, something of his spirit or character survives in the magic of his 'glowing golden' (p.58) pelt, which for Thurston Hough is 'my sole comfort in these troubling times … Even to gaze upon its wondrous lustre lifts my spirits' (p.64). When Levi takes ownership of the pelt after prying it from Hough's grotesque fingers, the pelt fills him with 'confidence and a renewed sense of purpose' (p.158). Even in the face of another death, this time quite horrific (the gory descriptions of Hough are nothing like the mystical, gentle descriptions of the McAllister women in 'Ash'), the pelt 'lives' on, in a different form than in its previous life. Indeed, it is key in the resolution of the novel; the smell of the burning pelt prompts the Cloud God to unleash the storm over Notley Fern Gorge, vanquishing the last of the fire.

Another illustration of the impermanence of death is in Jack's story, as he gradually learns that while an individual fire may be put out – 'in a swift moment he changed from a crackling god into a blinking, dying ember, spewing out his final breaths in a thin strand of smoke' (p.168) – this does not mean the end for him; 'he did not die; he merely slept' (p.168). From then on, he 'sleeps' and 'awakes' many times, over hundreds of years. As well as sidestepping death, he involuntarily passes his essence to his baby daughter by crying 'a tear of clean, unvarnished love', a 'drop of fire' (p.184). In this moment he hands down to Charlotte a power closely linked to his own, and ensures that part of him will continue to live on.

Loss and grief are felt not only by humans. An example is the Cloud God's sorrow at the disappearance of her 'waterlocked love', the 'other half' of her heart: the Esk God, with whom she has shared 'centuries of mutual, touchless adoration' (p.215). Though the Esk God's spirit survives in the power of his pelt, the fire in Notley Fern Gorge finally extinguishes this – 'the fur smoke that rose into her wisps and wafts from Notley confirmed it: he was dead' (p.215). The transience of the storm reflects not only 'a cloud's sorrow ... the hardest storms are made of sorrow' (p.216), but also Charlotte's and Levi's journeys and the hard storms of grief they have weathered.

Misunderstandings and self-knowledge

Key quotes

'I cannot express myself properly to him ...' (Charlotte, p.193)
'I consider myself a rational person, but my actions since our mother died weren't all that rational.' (Levi, p.219)

In order to illuminate the idea of connections and bonds, *Flames* explores how well characters understand themselves, and in turn how this might contribute to confusions either within or between characters. Some characters are not forthcoming, so it is only gradually that we learn what they know. In a kind of inversion of dramatic irony, the author is withholding from us information to which the characters have access. This can make such characters appear to be unreliable narrators because their stories seem to change. Charlotte provides an example: when she runs away, we are not initially sure exactly why, and we assume it is due to fear of Levi building a coffin. Yet much later, she tells us that she did not do it 'out of fear' (p.192) but because she was angry with him and did not want that to cause a rift in their relationship. She also admits that she 'was dreaming of leaving' before this because she sensed her flames 'crackling inside' (p.193). She was fully aware of this impending power – though she may not have known its full potential – but she misled us, so we did not know of that power until late in the story.

Several other characters demonstrate a knowledge of their motivations and emotional responses.

- **The detective**'s key motivations – to do her job successfully and be paid – are clear to both her and us, and are consistent throughout; she also knows perfectly well that her emotional detachment is a direct response to her fiancé's betrayal (p.84).
- **The Esk God** has a rock-solid belief in his own importance and power; we are likely to question this (since we first meet him simply as an ordinary water rat), but eventually the Cloud God corroborates the Esk God's confident assessment of his identity and place in the world. The magical powers of his pelt also support his view of himself as a deity.
- **Jack** tells his life story in great detail and scope, explaining his experiences (such as the physical feelings involved in taking on human form) and his desire for Edith and for their children. Nothing later in the novel contradicts his story.
- **Karl** understands well his relationship with his seal.

On the other hand, there are misunderstandings that prevent characters from seeing clearly or being able to maintain strong relationships. Most notable, perhaps, is Jack's relationship with his children. Edith is unable to forgive him for manipulating her, and his children are not able to forgive his disappearance following this, although they never actually understand why he abandoned the family and therefore cannot truly reconcile with him. In addition, they never know his true elemental identity and thus are not able to understand his motivations. This barrier prevents him from ever being able to truly express his love for them.

Similarly, Charlotte and Levi do not understand each other and, Charlotte asserts, have never had the kind of 'unconscious understanding' (p.192) that some siblings do. This fundamental disconnection, despite their strong love, means they cannot support each other in the wake of their mother's death. This is illustrated in 'Grove', when each expresses a desire to help the other (p.207), neither really knowing how. Levi's determination to finish the coffin stops him not only seeing how unwell he has become, but also recognising Charlotte's needs – which have nothing to do with being buried instead of cremated. He has believed from the beginning that he is helping her ('I cannot allow her pain to continue', p.51), but eventually questions himself: 'Did I really have what was best for Charlotte in the heart of my plans? ... I had failed her when she needed me most' (p.219). He is unable to determine his true motivations.

Levi is one of the characters who most clearly lacks insight into his own self. His decline into a kind of madness is a perfect representation of the extent to which he does not understand (is not even aware of) his own needs and true motivations. We have seen that others perceive Levi's struggles: Karl offers help; Jack visits to try to intervene, saying '*you're not healthy*' (p.164); and Charlotte, when she finds him, also offers help. But he persists in believing that there is nothing wrong. It is not until after the fire and the storm that Levi recognises that the way he'd treated his sister was not sensible, and it is only when he accepts the seal's touch that he arises fully from his 'murky' (p.219) state of existence and sees a future for himself.

Similarly, Allen's lack of self-awareness both facilitates and is a result of his wild, dangerous transformation, leading to pain not just for others but also for him. The reader can see what is occurring as he begins to merge with the cormorant, but it is never entirely clear if he knows what is happening. For example, what seems obvious to the reader as a physical transition from human to avian anatomy puzzles him. He describes in detail the way his nose has 'morphed ... into a much straighter protuberance' and 'has become harder too, almost bonelike' (p.117) but seems not to recognise it as a beak.

DIFFERENT INTERPRETATIONS

Different interpretations arise from different responses to a text. Over time, a text will evoke a wide range of responses from its readers, who may come from various social or cultural groups and live in very different places and historical periods. Responses by critics and reviewers can be published in newspapers, journals and books, both online and in print. They can also be expressed in discussions among readers in the media, classrooms, book groups and so on.

While there is no single correct reading or interpretation of a text, it is important to understand that an interpretation is more than a personal opinion – it is the justification of a point of view on the text. To present an interpretation of a text based on your point of view, you must use a logical argument and support it with relevant evidence from the text.

The critics' viewpoints

With a book as highly lauded as this, it can seem as if critics all have the same response: that the book is remarkable, masterful, exciting, engaging and so on. But by reading reviews and other responses to the text, you will pick up nuances, elements, themes and ideas you might not otherwise have noticed. Readers will always bring their own biases, context and expectations to a text, and these will influence individual interpretations, which is why it is important to read widely about a text you are studying, to help you shape your own interpretation.

So, even though critics may have responded positively to many of the same elements of this text, here are a few who have explored a very particular perspective, or focused on specific aspects.

Sarah Dempster for *The Sydney Morning Herald* and the reviewer 'KN' for *The Saturday Paper* both contextualise the novel with reference to other creative works, including paintings, film and literature, in order to help readers conceptualise the shifts in form and genre. Dempster (2018) says that the 'McAllister women evoke the eco-feminine figures that populate Renaissance art, such as Chloris in Botticelli's *Primavera,* who issues flowers as she transforms into the woodland-laden goddess', while KN (2018) notes that the novel is 'anchored in the genre of magical realism, recalling other first novels set in Tasmania, such as Richard Flanagan's *Death of a River Guide* and Tom Gilling's *The Sooterkin*', and alludes to 'a robust P. G. Wodehouse style' when discussing Thurston Hough.

Sam Jordison, for *The Guardian*'s semi-satirical 'Not the Booker prize' award series, dislikes magic realism, and claims that the novel 'asks for indulgence', proposing that an overview of the events might make *Flames* 'sound tangled and daft'. However, having declared this personal predisposition, he proceeds to analyse the book's successful elements, coming to the conclusion that it is 'solid, significant and emotionally resonant' and that he 'cared about the book' (Jordison 2019). It is worth reading this particular review, as it is a very balanced response, detailing what Jordison sees as the strengths and weaknesses of *Flames*. There are elements he admires (such as the devastating story of the seal's death) and elements he does not (such as the portrayal of Nicola and Charlotte's relationship, which he finds unconvincing and predictable) but, importantly, he provides detailed examples from the text – events, characters and themes – and short, relevant quotations to support each of his arguments.

A review by Jessie Neilson in the *Otago Daily Times*, a prominent independent New Zealand newspaper, concentrates less on genre and more on plot, briefly concluding that 'nowhere is safe, and everyone and everything seems to be on the run' (Neilson 2018). As a reviewer from outside Australia, Neilson generalises the setting, noting that 'the landscape is impeccably Australian with its wide, arid lands, yet otherworldly', rather than identifying its distinctive Tasmanian character. This illustrates how geographical as well as personal context can influence a reading of a novel. On the other hand, a review on a popular New Zealand news website, *Stuff*, takes the opposite perspective by focusing specifically on the novel's relationship with its place of origin, identifying the Tasmanian Gothic elements and offering a cross-Tasman perspective on Tasmanian cultural identity: reviewer Philip Matthews notes that 'we have a sense of Tasmania as darker, emptier and weirder than mainland Australia'. Matthews observes that the book culminates in 'a sense that a very strange place with its own mythology only needs to be tilted a little to become strange enough for fiction' (2018). Thus, geographical context does not always dictate responses to a text, but can influence them.

In a novel that is largely magic realist, interpretations of events, themes, characters and 'meaning' will vary widely. Elements may be taken literally (Allen really does transform into a human-cormorant hybrid; Charlotte really does 'leak' flame) or symbolically (both of these events are figurative representations of shifts in mental health). Further, when taken symbolically, readings may still differ: Allen's transformation may illustrate his decline into loneliness in an isolated environment or may be a self-blaming response to his grief and his belief that he is unable to protect the wombats; Charlotte's supernatural power might be an analogy for her recovering strength in the wake of grieving for her mother.

Two interpretations

Reading 1: *Flames* is a novel about destruction, grief and loss.

The main thread tying together the novel's many subplots is the grief shared by Charlotte and Levi McAllister; it sets the tone and links the other events. Charlotte and Levi are united in their grief yet also torn apart by misunderstanding each other's needs in moving through that grief. Being figuratively 'torn apart' leads to physical violence, such as Charlotte's spectacular fires and Levi's extreme attempts to finish the coffin, when he is found with an axe in Notley Fern Gorge. Physical destruction is an overwhelming motif throughout. Thurston Hough (who builds coffins – an innately grief- and loss-related pursuit) is gruesomely devoured by animals; a seal is butchered by orcas; wombats are violently murdered. These destructive incidents in the book are accompanied by grief: Karl does not fully recover from losing his seal – his 'other half' (p.14); the death of the wombats is devastating to Charlotte, Nicola and (for a time) Allen.

'Feathers', which charts first the wombat deaths and Allen's macabre transformation into a human-cormorant hybrid, is one of the more graphic illustrations of destruction in the novel. The wombats are not just dying but being violently murdered, and this provokes a deep, bodily grief for both Nicola and Charlotte: 'Nicola cries over the fresh corpses, Charlotte cannot look at them' (p.97). They feel their only option is to escape the situation by leaving the farm.

Loss is not always related to death, however. Charlotte and Levi lost a relationship with their father when he left (driven away by their mother after her discovery of a kind of emotional betrayal), and he in turn lost his right to paternal love and privilege. Neither children nor father have ever been able to come to terms with this fracturing of their family, so all are still dealing with the grief, in their own ways. Yet still, death and loss are frequently paired. For example, the final pages of the novel hint that perhaps Jack has somehow died his last death: he is 'small among the ferns. Lonely in the flames', and he 'releases a long, heavy sigh. His eyes are closed' (p.212). While not explicit, these actions speak of a sad resignation to an unwanted fate.

Even incidental characters and wider events are driven by loss and grief. The detective links her emotional coldness to the infidelity of her fiancé, while the monumental storm is a direct response to the final destruction of the Cloud God's love, the Esk God, when she smells 'the smoke that fizzed out of a small, golden-brown pelt in the heart of the fire' (p.215).

Reading 2: In the novel *Flames*, love and nurturing are what matter.

In the face of terrible grief, danger, fear and sorrow, many characters in *Flames* show one another compassion, which helps them survive. The novel begins with the death of Edith (mother of Levi and Charlotte), and immediately Levi formulates a plan to ease Charlotte's suffering in the long term by preventing her being cremated and returned to life like many of their female relatives. He sees her pain and, believing she has 'fears about her own death', does everything he can to build her a coffin designed to 'put some of these fears to rest' (p.51). Although ultimately we learn that his intentions were misaligned with her needs, his persistence in his plan shows his dedication to nurturing the wellbeing of his sister. In turn, she runs away from him to avoid hurting him, and when they eventually reunite in Notley Fern Gorge, she feels a 'rushing tide of worry' for him and tells him *'I'll find you some help'* (p.207).

The relationship between Charlotte and Nicola emerges out of compassion for each other in the face of Allen's increasing and treacherous madness. They establish a cautious friendship, 'a friendship defined by shared danger' (p.140). When they begin to grow afraid, a new closeness develops between them: 'their dining chairs practically bump legs at the table, and it has become a rare sight to see them alone' (p.101); they stick together, 'making sure each knew where the other was' (p.140). Shortly before they evacuate, Nicola inadvertently discovers that she can halt Charlotte's fire just by touch. She then takes on the role of protector, taking Charlotte to Cradle Mountain and keeping watch over her at all times, ready to relieve her of accidental flame.

Similarly, there are nurturing cross-species relationships. For example, Karl and his seal share a mutual concern. They are more than just hunting partners; they share an emotional bond. In the attack on the seal, the two show great care for each other even though ultimately neither is able to prevent the death. Karl attempts to keep the orcas back with his spear, 'trying to keep eyes on them all' despite knowing that 'orcas don't attack humans' (p.17). This shows that his concern is for his seal, who in turn worries for him, 'spinning around him' (p.17) so that Karl soon realises he is 'being protected' (p.18).

QUESTIONS & ANSWERS

This section focuses on your own analytical writing on the text, and gives you strategies for producing high-quality responses in your coursework and exam essays.

Essay writing – an overview

An essay on a literary work is a formal and serious piece of writing that presents your point of view on the text, usually in response to a given topic. Your 'point of view' in an essay is your interpretation of the meaning of the text's language, structure, characters, situations and events, supported by detailed analysis of textual evidence.

Analyse – don't summarise

In your essays it is important to avoid simply summarising what happens in a text.

- A **summary** is a description or paraphrase (retelling in different words) of the characters and events. For example: 'Macbeth has a horrifying vision of a dagger dripping with blood before he goes to murder King Duncan.'
- An **analysis** is an explanation of the real meaning or significance that lies 'beneath' the text's words (and images, for a film). For example: 'Macbeth's vision of a bloody dagger shows how deeply uneasy he is about the violent act he is contemplating, and conveys his sense that supernatural forces are impelling him to act.'

A limited amount of summary is sometimes necessary to let your reader know which part of the text you wish to discuss. However, always keep this to a minimum and follow it immediately with your analysis of what this part of the text is really telling us.

Plan your essay

Carefully plan your essay so that you have a clear idea of what you are going to say. The plan ensures that your ideas flow logically, that your argument remains consistent and that you stay on the topic. An essay plan should be a list of **brief dot points** covering no more than half a page.

- Include your central argument or main contention – a concise statement of your overall response to the topic.
- Write three or four dot points for each paragraph, indicating the main idea and evidence/examples from the text. Note that in your essay you will need to *expand* on these points and *analyse* the evidence.

Structure your essay

An essay is a complete, self-contained piece of writing. It has a clear beginning (the introduction), middle (several body paragraphs) and end (the last paragraph or conclusion). It must also have a central argument that runs throughout, linking each paragraph to form a coherent whole. See examples of introductions and conclusions in the 'Analysing a sample topic' and 'Sample answer' sections.

The introduction establishes your overall response to the topic. It includes your main contention and outlines the main evidence you will refer to in the course of the essay. Write your introduction *after* you have done a plan and *before* you write the rest of the essay.

The body paragraphs argue your case – they present evidence from the text and explain how this evidence supports your argument. Each body paragraph needs:

- a strong **topic sentence** (usually the first sentence) that states the main point being made in the paragraph
- **evidence** from the text, including some brief quotations
- **analysis** of the textual evidence, with **explanation** of its significance and how it supports your argument
- **links back to the topic** in one or more statements, usually towards the end of the paragraph.

Connect the body paragraphs so that your discussion flows smoothly. Use some linking words and phrases such as 'similarly' and 'on the other hand', though don't start every paragraph like this. Another strategy is to use a significant word from the last sentence of one paragraph in the first sentence of the next.

Use key terms from the topic – or synonyms for them – throughout, so the relevance of your discussion to the topic is always clear.

The conclusion ties everything together and finishes the essay. It includes strong statements that emphasise your central argument and provide a clear response to the topic.

Avoid simply restating the points made earlier in the essay – this will end on a very flat note and imply that you have run out of ideas and vocabulary. The conclusion should be a logical extension of what you have written, not just a repetition or summary of it. Writing an effective conclusion can be a challenge. Try using these tips:

- Start by linking back to the final sentence of the second-last paragraph – this helps your writing to flow, rather than leaping back to your main contention straight away.
- Use synonyms and expressions with equivalent meanings to vary your vocabulary. This allows you to reinforce your line of argument without being repetitive.
- When planning your essay, think of one or two broad statements or observations about the text's wider meaning. These should be related to the topic and your overall argument. Keep them for the conclusion, since they will give you something 'new' to say but still follow logically from your discussion. The introduction will be focused on the topic, but the conclusion can present a wider view of the text.

Essay topics

1 *'Flames* shows that it is not possible to entirely control one's own future.' Discuss.

2 "I'd been burning ever since our mother had."
Discuss the use of fire in the novel.

3 *'Flames* is a symbolic portrait of a real world.' Discuss.

4 'The characters in *Flames* are all at points of desperation.'
To what extent to you agree?

5 How does Arnott use genre to influence the interpretation of his themes?

6 'In *Flames,* animals and the environment reflect the human characters' emotions.' Discuss.

7 How does *Flames* use narrative perspective to construct relationships between characters?

8 'In *Flames,* death is not the enemy.' Discuss.

9 *'Flames* is about transformation.'
To what extent do you agree?

10 "I wanted to feel close to her, to feel like she and I were almost interchangeable ..."
Discuss the role of connection in *Flames.*

Vocabulary for writing on *Flames*

Anthropomorphism: attributing human forms, behaviours or motivations to non-human beings such as animals, gods or (less commonly) inanimate objects. Anthropomorphism and personification are very similar, but anthropomorphism usually refers to human-like characterisation of living beings or deities (animal characters in children's stories are a good example) while personification attributes human characteristics to inanimate objects or abstract ideas. (See also ***Personification*** and ***Pathetic fallacy***; the three concepts are closely linked.)

Dehumanisation: the opposite of anthropomorphism. This is used in 'Feather' when Allen begins to become less and less 'human', at the same time becoming more cruel and dangerous. Dehumanisation of a character encourages us to view them with less empathy. However, in this chapter, anthropomorphism is simultaneously used to humanise the cormorant, so the two techniques overlap in an interesting way.

Pastiche: a work of art that borrows motifs from other creative works. In literature, this generally refers to the imitation or harnessing of multiple genres and styles, as Arnott does in *Flames*. The word is sometimes used as a criticism, but is not inherently negative.

Pathetic fallacy: ascribing human emotions or behaviour to non-human, non-sentient forms of nature. The novel uses many instances of pathetic fallacy. An example is the Cloud God, who feels a very human kind of attachment to the Esk God, and in the book's climax experiences devastating sorrow.

Personification: ascribing human characteristics to inanimate objects or abstract ideas or concepts, or representing objects or ideas as humans (such as representing justice as a woman holding scales). An example from the novel is 'small towns have a habit of keeping quiet' (p.85).

Therianthropic: a description of an entity that combines the form of an animal and a human, or shifts between the two. Jack and Allen both embody this concept. It is related to anthropomorphism and personification, in the sense of drawing together the human and the non-human, but a therianthropic representation relates to myth; it is not a literary technique.

Analysing a sample topic

'*Flames* shows that it is not possible to entirely control one's own future.' Discuss.

Always approach an essay prompt with an open mind; don't try to apply your existing theories or quotes before properly exploring the topic. You might choose to start by making sure you understand the key words. Alternatively, you might decide to begin by brainstorming initial responses to the topic, and then refining these to make sure you have considered all elements, key words and implied ideas (such as, here, the assumption that to control one's future is desirable). At this stage, it can also be helpful to rewrite the topic in your own words.

In this topic, an important word is 'control' – you'll need to define this for yourself (though that definition will probably not be included in your actual essay). The word is a simple one, but consider nuances and associations; use dictionaries and thesauruses to widen your interpretation of the word. Similarly, consider 'entirely': this key word invites you to explore both sides of an argument. The word 'future' asks you to think about characters' journeys.

It can be useful to brainstorm broader ideas – ideas not tied to the text – that relate to words in the prompt. An example might be brainstorming around the key word 'future', which could mean expectations and hopes of good things yet to come; a sign of consequences that are impending or events already set in motion; or a shift away from the past. 'Future' might also be associated with ideas like change, growth and maturity. The word often has positive connotations, but can also carry notions of fear, trepidation and anxiety.

Once you have a detailed understanding of the topic, it's time to form your contention – your interpretation of the topic in relation to the text. In a 'discuss' topic, you aren't expected to agree or disagree with the prompt, but rather to show your understanding of the text by forming a contention and supporting it with relevant examples and analysis of events, characters, settings, themes and techniques.

Sample introduction

In Robbie Arnott's *Flames,* a series of subplots (in various genres) combine into one main narrative; characters in the subplots are frequently portrayed as having limited authority over their own lives, and together these characters contribute to a wider textual perspective on personal agency. While characters may make choices, often the outcomes are thwarted or complicated by those around them – sometimes to the point that individuals are under others' control. The ideas explored through these interactions between characters include power, fate and independence, and the overwhelming evidence in the text is that it is impossible to maintain full control over one's own fate.

Body paragraph outline

Paragraph 1: To be in control involves making decisions that lead to desired outcomes; often characters do not have the opportunity to make those decisions.

- Karl does not choose his seal – he waits for one to choose/accept him.
- The Esk God, despite being a deity, cannot see his 'creator', the Cloud God; nor can he escape Thurston Hough's cage (later, though, his pelt exerts control over others such as Levi and Hough).
- When the detective first tries to approach Jack, she can't: 'I stopped … not of my own accord' (p.92).
- Evidence from minor characters: the Last Graham's wife 'changes the locks' (p.87) and takes their 'kids, house, kayak, everything' (p.72); Louise requires the seal's approval to marry Karl.

Paragraph 2: Larger-scale examples of this lack of control have far-reaching consequences.

- Jack is prevented from rebuilding his relationship with his children: 'he haunted Levi and Charlotte … but Edith had forbidden him from going near them' (p.188).
- Charlotte has no power over her dangerous flames, though she spends time 'trying to summon' and 'trying to control them' (p.152).
- Although the detective has chosen to live alone, emotionally detached, her past (specifically her fiancé) has shaped her future.

Paragraph 3: The text sometimes complicates the notion of control and clear decision-making, as shown in Allen's story.

- Allen describes pleasure at merging with the cormorant – 'a feeling of calmness settled over me. Control, finally, had been restored' (p.108). But does he really have control, or is the cormorant (or what it symbolises) ultimately in control?
- The imagery suggests that he is not in control: he is 'directed by the tapping of the bill on my breastbone' (p.112); he notes that 'the glorious cormorant's wings were fanning at the back of my knees, lending me unnatural speed' (p.113).

Paragraph 4: Characters are clearly under Jack's control.

- Jack tinkers with 'lighting tiny sparks in their minds' so others 'look upon him favourably'; he lit 'other sparks, deeper sparks' that 'meddled with their ability to perceive him clearly' (p.176).
- He manipulated Edith's emotions so that she fell in love with him, resulting in their marriage and the births of their children.
- One interpretation is that Levi is under his father's spell for the entire story; he only realises his motivations were 'murky, as if they were someone else's' (p.219) after his father's death.

Sample conclusion

Again and again in *Flames,* we see others interfering with characters' intentions – whether purposefully or not. Goals, motivations and desires are often impeded, sometimes in small and temporary ways, but at other times in particularly insidious and life-changing ways. Although the various genres in the novel can influence the representations of control (for example, the use of magic realism means there are questions as to what is 'true' and what is not), in each case the outcome is the same. The fact that the same developmental patterns affect multiple characters in multiple sections of the novel strongly illustrates the fact that people can never be completely responsible for their own fortunes.

SAMPLE ANSWER

"I'd been burning ever since our mother had."
Discuss the use of fire in the novel.

The idea of fire is represented everywhere in Robbie Arnott's *Flames*: through events, relationships, themes and setting. The text is full of both literal and symbolic fire, and these representations work in parallel, sometimes through the same event or character, to develop and heighten the impact of the narrative. Arnott uses fire to construct and convey every important element of the novel – structure, plot and emotional impact. The quote 'I'd been burning ever since our mother had' occurs late in the book, and thus summarises the ongoing contribution the idea of fire makes to characters' lives as well as to readers' interpretations of the stories in *Flames*.

A literal flame, the cremation of Levi and Charlotte's mother, opens the novel and provides the inciting incident for the central narrative: Levi's quest to build a coffin so that Charlotte never has to undergo the trauma of cremation and resurrection. This drives Charlotte's desire to flee (as well as, we ultimately learn, her desire to escape her own flames, inherited from her father). Thus, fire is used as an important structural device to progress the plot. This is enhanced by the regular appearance of fire at significant points in the novel, including the resurrected Edith McAllister self-immolating on Jack's lawn, the Esk God's dream of fire when he takes shelter with Charlotte, the fire at Melaleuca and the fire at Notley Fern Gorge. Using fire as a recurring motif is one of the ways in which Arnott draws together the text's various subplots.

The language choices in *Flames* are concerned with creating strong imagery – often tied to the natural environment – and constructing a vivid world where objects, characters and events, through figurative language, become hyperreal and dramatic. This is perhaps most notable in descriptions related to fire. Examples include concise images such as 'hugest land-scouring flames' and 'a fat globule of blueberry fire', and more descriptive passages such as 'a bursting lick of brightness … a tongue of yellow-orange fire that grew and danced and rose, chewing up the leaf nest and spitting out black char'. The extended portrayals of the two dramatic fires (at Melaleuca and at Notley Fern Gorge), as well as much of Jack's history in 'Coal', similarly rely on descriptive, sensory and figurative language to convey the physical as well as emotional experience of burning, flame and fire.

This imagery contributes to the overall tone of the novel, in which compelling and constant description emphasises the emotional connections between characters as well as developing the settings, events, conflicts and, ultimately, resolutions. As a strong component of the novel's main genre of magic realism, imagery of fire (and other natural phenomena such as the flood, along with supernatural events such as Allen's transformation) is sometimes concrete and sometimes not, and often lies somewhere in between. For example, Jack's description of his life as fire is often very literal: 'he took a wallaby … in his coals and singed off its fur, melted its tendons and burned its flesh'. At other times, it is less so: 'he learned more and burned hotter'. Similarly, Charlotte's experience with fire is not a naturalistic event but is perfectly natural within the world of the novel. Her fire is literal – it physically burns the wombat farm, part of Notley Fern Gorge and Nicola's skin. It is also symbolic – she experiences a loss of control when she begins 'leaking fire', representing her loss of emotional control. Jack's and Charlotte's roles in the narrative catalogue relationships between humans, between fire and humans, and between fire and the landscape. Thus Arnott implicitly creates a strong link between humans and the environment – a central idea in the book.

Another central idea is alienation, along with its inverse: the notion of closeness between two beings – even non-humans, as in the case of the Esk God and the Cloud God (the emotional climax is the storm initiated by the Cloud God in response to the Esk God's burning pelt). One of the illustrations of the human desire to ally with another is the relationship between Charlotte and Nicola – a relationship intimately tied to fire, from the symbolic ('the burn that spread from [Nicola's] stomach the first time she touched Charlotte McAllister') to the literal (Charlotte's combustion: *'You stop doing it when I touch you'*). Fire is what brings them emotionally – and, eventually, sexually – close, and in the climactic scene in Notley Fern Gorge, it is what almost tears them apart but instead cements their partnership. Surviving the fire together seems to eliminate Charlotte's intentions of leaving Nicola, as 'their foreheads fell to rest against one another'. The women's relationship is based on an unusual symbolism: while fire is often associated with love (burning desires, hearts aflame, fiery romance), here Nicola suppresses Charlotte's fire. This might suggest exactly the opposite of love, but the connection provides safety and comfort for both, and each time Nicola puts out Charlotte's fire, the two grow closer. Nicola, as well as quenching Charlotte's fire, is helping to settle the tensions, fears and grief that manifest as flames in Charlotte.

While not everything in *Flames* is directly tied to fire, it has a pervasive presence in the text, and most characters, relationships and ideas can be traced back to fire in various forms. The many stories are connected through the motif of fire, transforming them from disparate plots into one unified narrative. The frequent descriptive language used to convey the sense and meaning of burning makes the device one that contributes significantly to the overall tone of the novel, in which there is frequent danger as well as a mesmerising quality, just as flames can have. Characters such as Charlotte and Jack are central in carrying the theme and imagery of fire throughout the novel, but through them, incidental moments, relationships, crises and resolutions are ignited, resulting in a book that burns as consistently as its title promises.

REFERENCES & READING

Text

Arnott, Robbie 2018, *Flames*, Text, Melbourne.

Other resources

Atkinson, Sam (ed.) 2016, *The Literature Book*, Dorling Kindersley, London. (Offers a useful, simple introduction to a variety of literary genres.)

Cuddon, JA 1999, *The Penguin Dictionary of Literary Terms and Literary Theory*, Penguin Books, Victoria.

Doolan, Emma 2019, 'Australian Gothic: From Hanging Rock to Nick Cave and Kylie, This Genre Explores Our Dark Side', *The Conversation*, 4 July, https://theconversation.com/australian-gothic-from-hanging-rock-to-nick-cave-and-kylie-this-genre-explores-our-dark-side-111742 (A brief, enlightening examination of the Australian Gothic tradition.)

Reviews

Dempster, Sarah 2018, 'A Mythic Reimagining of Small-town Australia', *The Sydney Morning Herald*, 8 June, https://www.smh.com.au/entertainment/books/a-mythic-reimagining-of-smalltown-australia-20180529-h10p2t.html

Jordison, Sam 2019, 'Not the Booker: *Flames* by Robbie Arnott Review: Magic Works in a Wild Tasmania', *The Guardian*, 19 August, https://www.theguardian.com/books/booksblog/2019/aug/19/not-the-booker-flames-by-robbie-arnott-review-magic-works-in-a-wild-tasmania

KN 2018, 'Robbie Arnott: *Flames*', *The Saturday Paper*, May 19–25, https://www.thesaturdaypaper.com.au/2018/05/31/flames/15266520006247

Matthews, Philip 2018, 'Book Review: *Flames,* by Robbie Arnott', *Stuff*, 1 July, https://www.stuff.co.nz/life-style/105010736/book-review-flames-by-robbie-arnott

Neilson, Jessie 2018, 'Fairy Tale Embedded into Australia', *Otago Daily Times*, 2 July, https://www.odt.co.nz/entertainment/books/fairy-tale-embedded-australia